QUALITY DEER MANAGEMENT

THE BASICS AND BEYOND

TEXT AND PHOTOGRAPHY BY

CHARLES J. ALSHEIMER

Published by

krause
publications
The World's Largest Hobby & Collectibles Publisher

Please call or write for a free catalog of publications. Our address is 700 E. State St., Iola, WI 54990-0001. The toll-free number to place an order or to request a free catalog is (800) 258-0929, or use our regular business number (715) 445-2214.
Library of Congress Catalog Number: 2002105096
ISBN: 0-87349-335-4
Printed in the United States of America

*For these very special people who have inspired
and enriched my quality deer management journey.*

Aaron Alsheimer
Dr. Gary Alt
Heffner Appling, Sr.
Bob and Alma Avery
Erwin Bauer
Mike Biggs
Al Brothers
Bentley Brown
Dr. Craig Dougherty
Paul Daniels
Pat Durkin
Joe Hamilton
Haas Hargrave
George Harmes
George and Elizabeth Jambers
Ben Lingle
Dr. Mike Lormore
Brian Murphy
Rob Roote
Dan Schmidt
Ray and Steve Scott
Dr. Grant Woods
John Wootters
Bob Zaiglin

Table of Contents

Foreword

Not too many people get to live out the dream of meeting their childhood heroes, so I guess that makes me one of the lucky ones.

Sometime in April 1981, my eighth-grade English teacher asked my class to write about our career objectives. Mine was short and to the point: "I love to write stories, especially about hunting. So, when I grow up, I want to work for a magazine like *Deer & Deer Hunting*."

Why *D&DH*? I can't remember the exact reason, but I do know my aspirations had a lot to do with the contributions by field editor Charles J. Alsheimer. His deer-hunting insights were so valuable that I actually cut them out of the magazines and kept them in a three-ring binder (one that was supposed to be used for my science-class projects). I found his photos equally fascinating, and they soon found places on my bedroom walls next to posters of baseball stars George Brett, Gorman Thomas, Dave Winfield and Carl Yastrzemski.

Fast-forward 14 years. After earning a bachelor's degree in journalism and spending more than four years cutting my teeth at newspapers and a non-hunting magazine, I caught a break and landed the *D&DH* associate editor position.

Within a week, I found myself fielding a telephone call from "Charlie" Alsheimer.

I was instantly starstruck. My deer-hunting hero was no longer a typewritten name or a timeless photograph. The excitement only escalated when, in September 1995, Alsheimer traveled to Wisconsin for a meeting of the magazine's field editors. In fact, during that trip, he photographed me with my first bow-kill. Talk about a thrill. I might as well have been throwing batting practice to Rod Carew.

The rest, as they say, is history. Over the next seven years, Alsheimer and I forged a special friendship. Although I now admire his work more than ever, I've learned he's the genuine article when it comes to white-tailed deer and deer hunting. He might not be considered a deer researcher in the scientific community's collective mind, but make no mistake: Alsheimer's insights on deer behavior and whitetail management evolved from more than 30 years of intense field work and trial-and-error experiments.

Alsheimer literally lives and breathes deer hunting. Need proof? Well, in 1973, he and his wife bought a nondescript farm. Although the land held some whitetails, it was anything but a prime hunting property. Over the years, however, Alsheimer's hard work and desire transformed the farm into a model QDM property. After implementing sound deer-harvest and forestry-management practices, Alsheimer soon became a master at analyzing properties and prescribing no-fail QDM plans.

Of course, he won't take all the credit for his QDM successes. In fact, Alsheimer diverts much of the credit to Al Brothers, the Texas-based whitetail guru who many consider the "father of QDM." After spending time with Brothers in Texas in the late 1980s and learning about the benefits of habitat and herd management, Alsheimer took the ideas home and implemented them on his property. The result was nothing short of phenomenal. His property literally went from a good deer-hunting parcel to a whitetail paradise.

Alsheimer will be the first to admit there are no quick fixes for implementing long-term QDM programs. In other words, a sound program involves a lot more than merely dropping some clover seeds in a freshly tilled plot and passing up young bucks during the hunting seasons.

That's the reason for this book. If you're interested in growing bigger and healthier whitetails, you'd be best served to absorb every word on these pages.

You needn't look any further than Alsheimer for the answers to your whitetail questions.

Daniel E. Schmidt
Deer & Deer Hunting *editor*
January 2002

Introduction

For more than 10 years, I've been immersed in QDM. I'll have to admit there were times in the beginning when I wasn't sure I was doing the right thing. This stemmed from skeptical reactions from fellow New Yorkers and the slow pace of the program.

Traditions die hard in the Northeast, and the thought of managing land for quality deer was not an idea that was embraced by many New Yorkers a decade ago. Despite the drawbacks, I kept the vision. Early on, progress was almost indistinguishable. But as the years passed, QDM gained momentum and acceptance when the public began to see results.

In assessing QDM's successes, I can't help but think of the 2001 deer season, which was truly one to remember on our farm. In many ways, it began with the 2000 deer season.

The 2000 season was the first in four consecutive years that I didn't kill a buck on our farm. One of my QDM goals is to hunt $3\frac{1}{2}$-year-old or older bucks, and in 2000 I couldn't get one in my sights. I did pass up many yearlings and several $2\frac{1}{2}$-year-old bucks. On five occasions, I passed a beautiful $2\frac{1}{2}$-year-old 8-pointer — twice in archery season and three times during gun season.

In February, my son found one of the 8-pointer's sheds in a food plot on our farm, and a neighbor who practices QDM found the other in one of his food plots. So, expectations ran high when the 2001 archery season opened in October.

Throughout this past summer, we planted and worked food plots. Scouting sessions also revealed several nice bucks that I guessed were at least 3 years old. The excitement built as autumn approached.

During the first two weeks of archery season, the only opportunities I had were on yearling and $2\frac{1}{2}$-year-old bucks. I passed all of them. Then on the morning of Nov. 1, I was treated to what I call a "November moment." Shortly after 8 a.m., the woods exploded as six bucks chased and fought over an estrous doe that had bedded 35 yards from my stand. For several minutes, the woods resonated with snorts, grunts and snort-wheezes as the bucks tried to sort out who was going to do the breeding. The action ended as fast as it had started when a yearling buck spooked the bedded doe and she ran from sight with all the bucks in hot pursuit. Of the six bucks, only one fit my definition of a shooter. The other five included four yearlings and a $2\frac{1}{2}$-year-old 8-pointer.

Despite my disappointment at not getting a chance at the big buck, I knew the rut was intensifying, and I hoped to get another crack at him before the season ended. Nearly two weeks later, after passing up other bucks, my chance came.

Shortly after daylight on Nov. 10, the big buck returned to the same location. This time he was alone, and I was ready for him. With his nose to the ground, he came down a trail that passes my stand and stopped to work the mock licking branch I had hung. As he feverishly worked the branch, I slowly came to full-draw, placed my 10-yard pin behind his front shoulders and released the arrow. The buck bolted at the arrow's impact and ran through the thick hardwoods. After anxiously waiting for 45 minutes, I picked up the blood trail and recovered the buck after an easy 200-yard tracking session.

While running my fingers over the buck's antlers, I was struck by how similar they were to the sheds my son and neighbor had found in February. The following day, when we compared the sheds to the buck's rack, everything was confirmed. It was the same buck I had passed up five times in 2000. From 2000 to 2001, the buck's antlers had grown from 110 inches to 140 inches Boone and Crockett.

After killing the buck, I figured the chances of

killing another buck of this caliber were over for the year. I was wrong. For the first two and a half weeks of our gun season, I killed does and passed several yearling and $2^1/_2$-year-old bucks. Then on Dec. 9, while hunting from the only ground blind on our farm, I received an early Christmas present.

Late in the afternoon, with nearly 40 turkeys, five bucks and 13 does and fawns within 75 yards of my stand, I killed a big 8-pointer. He was a perfect 8-pointer with nearly 12-inch G-2s that would qualify as a trophy nearly anywhere in North America. Ironically, I had never seen the buck before that afternoon, which means he probably wandered in from surrounding QDM property.

Reliving these events leaves me amazed and a bit in awe. It's been an incredible year, and a testimony to what has transpired in the past 10 years. The days of dreaming about hunting quality bucks on our New York farm are over. In the past decade, our area has gone from the "land of the yearlings" to the "land of possibilities" — thanks to QDM.

Contrary to what some might think, QDM is not rocket science. The beauty of the concept is that it's not complicated, and it can work wherev-er whitetails are found, if it's given a fair chance.

This book is not meant to be a technical manual about QDM. There are already several excellent QDM books like this on the market. Rather, I wanted to share through my photos and experiences how QDM and the whitetail's story can be interwoven.

Though I've photographed and hunted other big-game animals throughout North America, I've never found a species that can stack up to the whitetail. In my mind, the white-tailed deer is the greatest big-game animal in North America. So, let me share the QDM journey with you. Also, dream a little. If you connect with the concept, you'll undoubtedly be struck by what QDM can offer when sound management is implemented.

As many sportsmen are finding out, the time is right for QDM. It is energizing, lets participants feel at one with nature and provides a wonderful way to become involved in growing better whitetails. As you are about to see, it's a win-win concept.

Charles J. Alsheimer
Bath, N.Y.
Dec. 27, 2001

CHAPTER 1

The History of QDM in North America

Deer hunting in North America has never been better than it is today. The whitetail population is flourishing, hunting equipment is more advanced than ever, and interest in deer management is at an all-time high. This interest stems from an explosion of ideas that greatly influenced landowners and hunters.

The modern era of deer management began with the post-World War II generation of deer biologists and hunters. The traditional approach to management that was widely used from the 1940s to the 1970s was far from perfect, but it laid the foundation for QDM, which has received a lot of attention in the past decade.

Needless to say, whitetail management in North America has been a journey. That journey hasn't always been easy, but it has included a great deal of change and a tremendous amount of progress.

A LOOK AT THE PAST

Before Europeans arrived in North America, natural predators and American Indians managed the whitetail population. By today's standards, American Indian harvest methods were unscientific. However, unlike the early Europeans who often looked at the dollar value of wildlife, American Indians viewed the whitetail and the rest of the natural world with reverence. They understood the balance of nature, and conse-

quently, they harvested only what they needed.

No one knows how many whitetails inhabited North America when Europeans arrived. Some estimate the deer population was as high as 40 million, while others claim it was less than the current population, which is estimated at more than 25 million. Regardless, whitetails were a prominent part of the North American landscape and a valuable form of sustenance for American Indians.

Archeological digs reveal that American Indians killed whitetails in all age classes. Whether this was planned or not, the American Indians were essentially practicing a natural form of QDM long before the Pilgrims landed at Plymouth. However, once Europeans gained a commercial foothold, things changed rapidly.

After the Revolutionary War, Americans became adventurous. They settled eastern North America and began moving westward. As prime whitetail habitat was cleared for farming and industry, the deer population fell significantly.

With open seasons, no bag limits and demand for venison in the cities, market hunting became popular in many parts of the East by the 1800s. As a result, the deer population plummeted, and by the late 19th century, less than 500,000 whitetails remained in North America.

Around 1900, a plea went out from conservation-minded sportsmen, and game seasons were closed throughout the country. Because of the

severity of mismanagement, it took decades for whitetails to recover.

By the time deer numbers returned to reasonable levels, the skill of deer hunting was nearly forgotten. This lack of knowledge made implementing a deer management program difficult. However, a more structured style of management — known today as traditional deer management — gradually took hold.

TRADITIONAL DEER MANAGEMENT

Traditional deer management was used to rebuild America's whitetail herds after the market-hunting era. It is still practiced today — at least in part — by many state game departments. In a nutshell, traditional management lets hunters kill antlered bucks while protecting all or part of the antlerless population. For the most part, bucks killed under traditional management programs are $1^1/_2$ years old. It's not uncommon for 80 percent to 95 percent of a state's antlered harvest to be yearlings under traditional management.

One principal goal of traditional management is to provide a huntable resource while keeping the deer population within the land's carrying capacity with little concern for how many bucks are killed. Traditional management worked well in its early years, but it has created myriad problems. Two of its biggest shortcomings are its tendency to overstress bucks and its inability to keep herds within the land's carrying capacity.

Despite its weaknesses, traditional management became popular because average hunters wanted to see a lot of deer. It certainly delivered in this concern throughout the years. In tradition-rich deer-hunting states like Michigan, Wisconsin, Pennsylvania, New York and Vermont, high deer populations provided hunters with the sightings they wanted. Unfortunately, many hunters didn't realize that traditional deer management was a time bomb.

Skyrocketing populations took a heavy toll on natural habitat. In many areas, this damage was

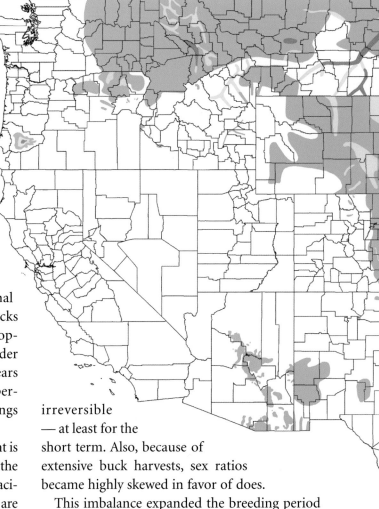

irreversible — at least for the short term. Also, because of extensive buck harvests, sex ratios became highly skewed in favor of does.

This imbalance expanded the breeding period because there weren't enough bucks to breed the does. The normal 40-day rut was stretched to 100 days in many states, placing a lot of stress on bucks. In addition, because of the extended breeding season, fawns were born later. In some cases, the traditional late May to early June birthing period stretched into August. Research shows that late fawns are smaller, have higher mortality rates and have poorer antler development as yearlings than fawns born on schedule.

QUALITY DEER MANAGEMENT

Though traditional management is still practiced in various forms, its problems have ushered in a new philosophy called quality deer management.

Before looking at how QDM began, it's important to understand what it is. The Quality Deer

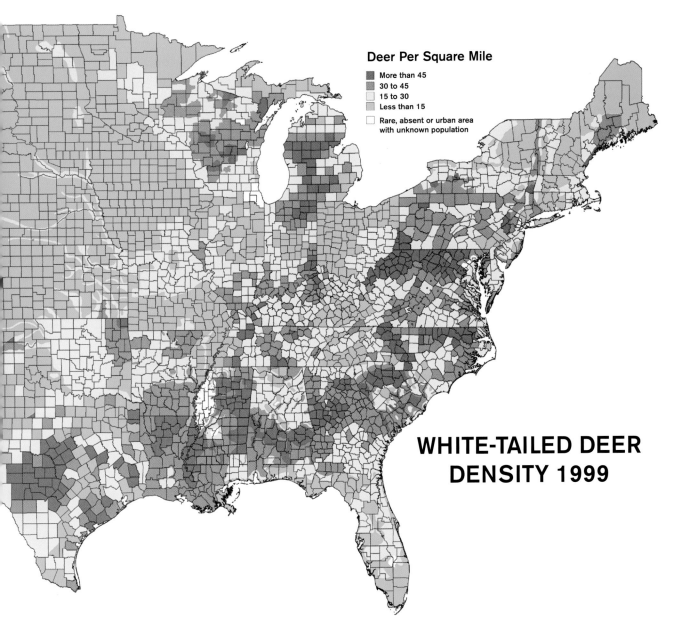

Deer Per Square Mile

- ■ More than 45
- ■ 30 to 45
- □ 15 to 30
- ■ Less than 15
- □ Rare, absent or urban area with unknown population

WHITE-TAILED DEER DENSITY 1999

Above: This map illustrates deer per square mile based on 1999 census data. Courtesy of the Quality Deer Management Association.

Management Association describes it this way: "QDM is a management philosophy/practice that unites landowners, hunters and resource managers in a common goal of producing biologically and socially balanced deer herds within existing environmental, social and legal constraints.

"This approach typically involves the protection of young bucks combined with an adequate harvest of female deer to maintain a healthy population in balance with existing habitat conditions and landowner desires. This level of deer management involves the production of quality deer (bucks, does and fawns), quality habitat, quality hunting experiences and quality hunters."

Many individuals have played a part in the modern QDM movement, and land managers and hunters have practiced QDM in various degrees for several decades. However, the movement began in the famed brush country of South Texas.

In the late 1960s and early 1970s, two Texas wildlife biologists, Al Brothers and Murphy E. Ray Jr., took a critical look at traditional management. Their concerns dealt with how traditional management protected does while embracing unregulated buck harvests.

After several years of formulating a more effective approach to deer management, they published their findings in a book called *Producing Quality Whitetails*, which put QDM concepts in print for the first time. The book was a huge success, and it challenged sportsmen to look closely at building a better deer herd.

Others were instrumental in spreading the concept Brothers and Ray introduced. In 1977, Texan John Wootters penned *Hunting Trophy Deer*. Like *Producing Quality Whitetails*, Wootters' work quickly sold out and became a classic. These two works laid the groundwork for modern QDM.

By the end of the 1970s, more individuals caught the QDM vision. Ray Scott, an avid

whitetail hunter and founder of Bass Anglers Sportsman Society, embraced the philosophy and began examining how he managed his Alabama property.

Scott, who later started the Whitetail Institute, recognized the relationship between antler growth and factors like age, nutrition and herd dynamics. He was one of the first to encourage using food plots as nutritional supplement. Since the early 80s, Scott has marketed many products for those interested in creating better deer habitat and promoted QDM through educational outlets. Today, nearly 750,000 deer hunters and landowners interested in building better whitetail herds read his publication, *The Whitetail News*.

About the same time Scott became interested in QDM, two South Carolina biologists, Joe Hamilton and Gerald Moore, played a key role in spreading the QDM message. In 1982, the South Carolina Wildlife and Marine Resources Department hosted the Southeast Deer Study Group in Charleston, S.C. Since then, the Southeast Deer Study Group has become the largest gathering of professional deer biologists and managers in the United States.

Al Brothers was the keynote speaker for the 1982 meeting. Brothers' speech challenged and encouraged biologists, managers and hunters to look at a new way of managing deer. In his presentation, Brothers asked, "Isn't it time we attempted to practice total deer management with regard to harvest by giving the antlered segment of the herd the same considerations as the antlerless segment?"

Brothers' remarks struck a cord and set the stage for the emergence of QDM. Shortly after his address, many Southern landowners and managers began to aggressively manage their deer

Top: Traditional deer management lets hunters see many deer and ample bucks. Unfortunately, the underharvesting of does and overharvesting of bucks has contributed to habitat destruction and excessive deer numbers. **Bottom:** Al Brothers and Murphy Ray Jr.'s book *Producing Quality Whitetails* is considered the bible of QDM. *Quality Whitetails* magazine is the official publication of the Quality Deer Management Association.

herds using QDM. The concept was successful in South Carolina. Unfortunately, it took longer to catch on in other parts of the country.

In October 1988, thanks to the efforts of Hamilton and many other individuals, the South Carolina Quality Deer Management Association was officially formed. Two and a half years later, the organization's scope was expanded with the creation of the national Quality Deer Management Association in May 1991.

The QDMA has grown considerably since then. Under the guidance of its current executive director, Brian Murphy, the organization has worked to educate the public on all aspects of QDM. Its publication, *Quality Whitetails*, is an outstanding source for those interested in QDM.

Above: Whitetails numbered 25 million when Europeans came to North America. However, because of open seasons, market hunting and loss of habitat, the population plummeted to 50,000 by the end of the 1800s. Thanks to sportsman, the carnage ended and populations were restored. Photo courtesy of Orville Hamman Jr.

THE ERA OF MEDIA

It wasn't until QDM was aggressively promoted that it caught on with mainstream sportsmen. During the past 10 years, wildlife biologists, outdoor writers and industry leaders have invested time and money to spread the message throughout the United States.

Cutting-edge whitetail magazines like *Deer & Deer Hunting* and *North American Whitetail* saw the benefits of managing for a quality herd and featured articles on the subject long before other pub-

lications. As a result, their readers saw the benefits and caught the vision of a better kind of deer management. Other publications have followed the lead of *Deer & Deer Hunting* and *North American Whitetail* in the past five years, resulting in an explosion of printed material dealing with QDM.

As the 21st century unfolds, QDM continues to gain the support of hunters and state wildlife agencies. The concept has become so popular that many states are considering incorporating portions of QDM into their deer management programs. From an entrepreneurial standpoint, dozens of companies have sprung up to handle the interest. In 30 short years, the concept has emerged from "something that can only work in Texas" to one that can and is working wherever it is tried.

Left: QDM places equal emphasis on antlered and antlerless deer.

nificantly different and should not be confused.

The primary objective of trophy deer management is to grow mature bucks older than 5 years that have high-scoring antlers. Achieving this with regularity requires ingredients that are not available to the average hunter. For starters, trophy management typically requires 5,000 or more acres. Because bucks tend to roam, even this is considered minimum. In addition, trophy deer management requires a selective buck harvest, a doe harvest that often exceeds QDM benchmarks and aggressive habitat management. Also, supplemental feeding programs are necessary for most successful trophy deer management programs.

These requirements make trophy deer management next to impossible in most areas. Because landowners need a lot of money to support this approach, it's generally limited to large ranches and high-fenced facilities. I've had the privilege of photographing on a few of these operations, and the deer they produce are truly impressive. Nevertheless, the cost of trophy deer management often exceeds its benefits.

Whitetail management has come a long way in the past century, but there is still much to be accomplished. As you will see in the following chapters, QDM offers the opportunity to substantially improve the whitetail population and create a fulfilling hunting experience in the process. ▪

TROPHY DEER MANAGEMENT

The subject of deer management would not be complete without mentioning another popular concept that is frequently confused with QDM. Trophy deer management has a small following among the hunting and management community. This form of management shares several objectives with QDM, but the two ideas are sig-

The Benefits of QDM

I t's Christmas in October, or so it seems. As I sit in my office, flipping through the stack of outfitter brochures on my desk, I feel like a child scanning a Sears, Roebuck and Co. *Wishbook*, dreaming of what Santa might bring. The present I'm wishing for has 12 points and weighs 300 pounds.

One brochure extols the virtues of a five-day Montana hunt for $2,800. Another touts the excitement of pursuing big-racked Alberta whitetails for only $3,500. A glitzy color booklet from a Texas outfitter falls out of the pile. This eye-catcher introduces "a place where the bucks are as big as Texas." The cost for the three-day hunt? Just shy of $6,000!

And so goes the rest of the stack — proof that the chance to hunt quality whitetails can be financially impossible for most hunters. How's that for a chunk of coal? The high cost of guided hunting is one reason so many sportsmen are seeking a different way to pursue quality whitetails.

THE BENEFITS OF QDM

In the past 10 years, thousands of deer hunters and landowners have discovered how fulfilling QDM can be. This chapter highlights six advantages of QDM, which can motivate you to develop your property and help sell QDM to fellow hunters.

A Feeling of Accomplishment: American deer hunters have a strong track record of giving more than they take. Through the years, sportsmen have used various methods to fulfill their obligation to the land. QDM is one of the most recent stewardship approaches to become popular with hunters.

QDM is a hands-on approach to whitetail management. It lets hunters become involved in all aspects of managing deer, from providing food to keeping the population within the land's carrying capacity. This increased involvement transforms the average hunter into a wildlife manager, which provides a greater sense of accomplishment. That satisfaction is what makes QDM so infectious.

Improved Adult-Doe-to-Antlered-Buck Ratio: For too long, traditional deer management has reigned in America. As outlined in the previous chapter, traditional management has several shortcomings, especially with doe management. When adult does outnumber antlered bucks more than 3-to-1, several problems occur. The rut becomes longer because there aren't enough antlered bucks to breed adult does. This places unnecessary stress on bucks and causes later fawn births the next spring.

In addition, high adult-doe-to-antlered-buck ratios decrease the rut's intensity. Consequently, when the ratio is greater than 3-to-1, rubbing, scraping, chasing and frenzied rutting behavior greatly diminish.

20 QDM: THE BASICS AND BEYOND

Above: In a well-managed QDM program, 1$^{1}/_{2}$-year-old bucks are protected. **Left:** By protecting yearlings and 2$^{1}/_{2}$-year-olds, bucks have a better chance of reaching maturity.

A sound QDM program emphasizes an adult-doe-to-antlered-buck ratio of less than 3-to-1. Most managers consider two does per buck attainable. When the ratio is 3-to-1 or lower, the entire herd benefits because the rut is condensed, fawns are born on schedule and antlered bucks endure less stress.

A liberal antlerless harvest is often needed to maintain a desirable doe population. Next to limiting the buck harvest, a restricted doe population is the most critical step in a successful QDM program. Chapter 9 will take a detailed look at this.

Improved Age Structure Among Bucks: Sportsmen often become involved in QDM because they want to see more mature bucks. To accomplish this, yearling buck harvests must be restricted. You won't see trophy antlers if yearlings don't reach maturity. By protecting younger bucks, landowners can nearly guarantee good things will happen. When bucks mature, the buck age structure is more diversified, which improves the rut's intensity. Restricted buck har-

vests also improve the sex ratio.

Improved Natural Habitat: After raising whitetails for several years and photographing them for more than three decades, I know they eat a lot. Research shows that a whitetail eats between 1¹/₂ to 2 tons of food per year, which my observations confirm. Of this, at least half comes from natural sources. In areas where most of a whitetail's diet comes from natural foods, the habitat can quickly be damaged or destroyed if deer numbers are not within carrying capacity. When natural habitat is inadequate, herd quality almost always diminishes. Inadequate food causes smaller antlers, fewer fawns and more disease.

QDM emphasizes bringing the herd within the land's carrying capacity, which protects habitat. Supplemental feeding areas, which are a major part of QDM, also decrease the stress on natural food and decrease crop damage, which is welcome news for farmers.

Improved Landowner/Hunter Opportunities: Hunters involved with QDM gain a greater appreciation for the land and wildlife. This, in turn, improves their relationships with landowners. When farmers and landowners understand that hunters want to improve the property, goodwill abounds.

Because QDM strives to control the doe population, hunters have more opportunities to kill animals. This aspect of QDM is particularly beneficial to young hunters because with success, they are more likely to enjoy hunting. In addition, QDM teaches young hunters about whitetail management.

Bonus Benefit: With QDM in place, hunters must address excess harvest. After all, you can only eat so much venison. In the past few years, a national organization called Farmers and Hunters Feeding the Hungry has established a network that lets hunters donate venison to needy families. In New York, the program is called Venison Donation Coalition. Such programs are tailor-made for QDM, and they let sportsmen give back to the community. For information on FHFH, call (301) 739-3000 or visit www.fhfh.org.

Left: With more mature bucks in the herd, the rut is more intense and includes more scraping, rutting and chasing. **Above**: QDM emphasizes antlerless harvest, which provides opportunities for young hunters.

PUTTING IT TOGETHER

After a program is up and running for a couple of years, the rewards are evident. The herd's genetic potential is revealed when hunters see and kill larger, more mature bucks. This can be dramatic in two to three years.

Because QDM participants know the herd's nutritional requirements, habitat improves as food plots are planted and natural food sources are restored. As with people, deer are what they eat. When better food sources are available, deer quality improves.

When a comprehensive QDM program is used, the herd's age structure improves. Even with the best genetics, habitat and management plan, better antlers are impossible without age. Bucks don't grow big racks because of a bag of seed or a block of minerals. If antlers are your goal, age is critical. Consequently, age, genetics, habitat and management must work in unison for a successful QDM program.

Of course, these benefits aren't possible if a program isn't implemented properly. When planning a program, you should consider everything from proper nutrition to determining how many deer should be killed. There is a lot to consider when starting a program, but when it comes together, you'll wonder why you didn't start sooner. ■

Right: When age, nutrition and management are addressed, whitetails flourish.

CHAPTER 3

Is QDM Feasible For You?

People often buy on impulse. If we have money, we buy things before considering what's required to run and maintain them. As with impulse buys, you can get in over your head with QDM if you're not careful.

When hunters and landowners watch a well-done presentation on QDM or see the caliber of bucks killed under QDM, their impulse is to jump in and start a program. Land and wildlife management is an energizing experience for some, but it can be a headache for others when they realize what it involves. This is why it's important to understand QDM in terms of land, time, money and equipment before making a decision.

WHAT ARE THE GOALS?

As I've lectured to hunters in the past few years, I've seen a shift from questions dealing with hunting strategies to ones concerning land management. Unlike 10 years ago, hunters are now asking about nutrition and growing a better deer herd. Though they might not realize it initially, these questions indicate they are interested in a form of QDM.

QDM means different things to nearly everyone. It is not a "one size fits all" concept, so questions vary. One question I often hear is: "I have a piece of property and wonder if it's possible to have a successful QDM program?"

Before answering, I ask questions to determine the person's goals. I try to find out the size of bucks he wants to hunt, whether he wants to see a lot of deer and whether he wants to improve habitat.

In most cases, those interested in QDM have similar goals. They want to hold deer on their land and have the potential to kill bigger bucks. Unfortunately, most landowners don't have the expertise to make that happen. Many are looking for a magic bullet that will provide immediate results. In reality, no such bullet exists. So, before offering answers, I ask questions, which makes it easier to steer someone in the right direction.

REQUIREMENTS

QDM requirements don't have to be overwhelming. Creating quality habitat is like exercising: Anything is better than nothing. Properties of all sizes can benefit from habitat improvement, increased doe harvests and restricted buck harvests. However, you need medium to large acreage to increase antler size.

Consider these factors.

Land Size: Most people assume that you must control at least 1,000 contiguous acres for QDM to be possible. Although this is great, many successful programs are run on much less land. The key is having neighbors who share your interests. If you do, QDM can be successful on any property. Eleven landowners

border our 215-acre farm. Of the 11, only four practice any form of QDM. If you viewed our farm and the surrounding properties from above — with the QDM properties darkened — you'd see a checkerboard pattern. Despite this, our QDM program has been successful.

Generally, you need 300 contiguous acres of quality deer habitat to get a program off the ground. This much land lets you properly lay out food plots and sanctuary locations and makes it easier to protect deer from landowners that don't practice QDM. For a QDM program to shine, you must plan where food sources, sanctuaries and other necessities will be positioned.

Some places, like small properties bordering public land and heavily hunted areas, aren't meant for QDM. You must also have adequate bedding cover. Land with only goldenrod fields or little brush and wooded land are not good candidates.

Sanctuary: A sanctuary is the backbone of a successful QDM program. At least one third of your property should be used as a sanctuary, which will become the property's prime bedding area. The most successful QDM programs usually have multiple sanctuaries.

Make sure no one enters the sanctuary during

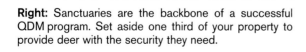

Right: Sanctuaries are the backbone of a successful QDM program. Set aside one third of your property to provide deer with the security they need.

hunting season. The goal of a sanctuary is to create the best accommodations for deer. You want the sanctuary to be so good that every deer for miles around will want to call it home.

My experience shows how effective a sanctuary can be. Each year, I've increased the number of sanctuary acres on our farm. Of 215 acres, 140 are currently designated as a sanctuary, which is more than 65 percent of the property. Because our area experiences intense hunting pressure during New York's firearms season, I've realized that the more land I keep off-limits to humans, the better the daytime deer activity will be on the rest of the property.

To enhance the sanctuary, I create structure by felling cull trees in September before the leaves fall. By doing this before leaf-off, I create a thick, tangled mess that deer love to bed in. With thick cover and no human intrusion, deer gravitate to the sanctuary area.

In the past two years, I've verified that properties with sanctuaries have greater deer movement than land with intense hunting pressure. Data collected by trail monitors revealed that on our QDM property, 58 per-

cent of deer activity during hunting season occurred during daylight. On land with heavy hunting pressure, less than 30 percent of activity was during the day. This is a huge testimony for QDM and the importance of an ample sanctuary and minimal hunting pressure. In most cases, a bigger sanctuary helps hold deer on your property, which translates to better hunting opportunities.

If your property is less than 300 acres and a wounded animal goes into the sanctuary, you must recover it at night. Use as few trackers as possible. In most cases, more than two is a crowd when tracking on QDM properties.

Night tracking eliminates the possibility of jumping deer and forcing them off the property. Through the years, I've found that when you jump a whitetail, it travels between 300 and 600 yards before stopping. On many QDM properties, a deer will vacate the property when spooked, leaving it at the mercy of surrounding landowners.

Food Plots: A minimum of 2 percent to 5 percent of your land should be earmarked for food plots. Food plots must be configured so deer will feel secure using them during the day. Food plots should also be situated so you can hunt near them without pressuring deer. Chapter 6 discusses food plots in detail.

Below: At least 2 percent to 5 percent of your property should be used as food plots.

HOW TO GET STARTED

If your dream is to have better deer hunting on your property, then QDM is the answer. However, one of the cornerstones of QDM is a thorough, well-thought plan.

The best way to get where you want in the least amount of time is to ask a professional. Many businesses throughout the country specialize in analyzing and setting up properties for QDM. In my part of the country, one of the best is North Country Whitetails.

Craig and Neil Dougherty of North Country Whitetails provide a variety of services pertaining to QDM. I asked Craig to explain how he responds to an inquiry.

Above: Water is the lifeblood of a QDM program. Without it, crops cannot flourish and deer won't grow to their potential.

"When someone contacts us, we ask a number of basic questions to find out what stage the interested party is in," he said. "It's also important to determine the individual's goals and objectives as early in the process as possible, so there is no wasted time.

"If the landowner has money in his budget and wishes to proceed, we do a feasibility study of the property to see if a QDM program is possible," he said. "One of the critical steps in setting up a program is establishing a

time line to show when things should get done. This provides a realistic way of looking at the whole project.

"Few people realize the length of time that's required to put a successful program together. In most cases, it takes at least four years to see the results landowners are looking for. So without a time line, an interested party can get very discouraged when things aren't going as fast as they think they should.

"The time line is determined by the number of people hours it will take to accomplish the task, as well as the dollars required to do it. Everyone wants the best bang for their buck, and planning helps to get you there. However, with many people, money is not the problem — time is. Unfortunately, many people don't commit themselves to meeting the time line. This is why good time management is necessary for a successful program.

"After the plan is in place, the landowner is ready to begin," Dougherty continued. "The first $500 should be spent on a chain saw and protective gear to be used to create natural habitat. After that, we encourage landowners to graduate to managing open spaces like road-

ways and fields, without turning over soil. You'd be amazed how a rotary mower and fertilizer can create green growth. After this, the normal progression is to cultivate the ground and plant food plots. You can do all this yourself or hire someone to do it for you."

COST FACTOR

As you might imagine, clearing land, building roads and planting food plots can be expensive. The Doughertys give these estimates to their clients.

Clearing Land: Many landowners must clear land for food plots. It takes a bulldozer about eight hours to clear one acre of brush and timber, which, depending on the region of the country and size of the dozer, will generally cost $75 to $100 per hour for a dozer and operator.

Food Plots: There are two ways to plant food plots — hire someone or do it yourself with your own equipment. Assuming the land is already cleared and you want to hire someone, it will take about four to six hours to plow, disk, lime (if needed), fertilize and seed the site for about $50 per hour. Lime costs up to $130 per acre, and fertilizer costs about $80 per acre. Seed costs vary,

Top left: Food plots can be expensive to create, so used equipment is usually the way to go. **Bottom left:** Make sure your food plots are easily accessible to deer and are placed where neighboring landowners can't take advantage of them.

but if you use clover, you will need about $30 to $45 of seed for one acre.

It costs about $650 per acre per year to till and replant your food plots. However, the cost of a food plot drops dramatically if you plant a perennial seed. If the seedbed is good and free of weeds, you should get three years out of a clover food plot, which makes it cost effective at an annual cost of less than $250 per acre.

Equipment Purchases: Many landowners who begin a QDM program eventually purchase their own equipment, which can be quite expensive. In most cases, new equipment is too costly, so used equipment is a better option. Below are estimates for items frequently used in QDM. Unless otherwise noted, the estimates are based on second-hand prices.

Utility tractor	$5,000 to $10,000
Two bottom plow	$250 to $500
8-foot disks	$250 to $500
Rotary mower	$250 to $2,500 (new)
Chain saw and protective gear	$350 to $600 (new)

Note: A light-duty professional or heavy-duty farm chain saw is adequate. You will also need chaps and headgear. Ear protection will prevent hearing loss and let you run the saw longer.

No cost analysis is complete without mentioning all-terrain vehicles. ATVs can be very useful for QDM, especially for landowners who cannot purchase or arrange to use farm equipment. On aver-

age, a quality ATV suitable for food plot work costs between $5,000 and $7,000. However, ATVs can only perform limited farming tasks with their attachments. They are not big enough or heavy enough to complete medium to large projects under certain terrain and soil conditions.

You can buy everything from plows to planters for your ATV. The Plotmaster, a popular ATV device, includes a drag, cultivator, adjustable disk harrow, plow attachment, elec-

tric seeder, cultipacker and carriage unit. It retails for about $3,000.

Above: On small- to medium-sized properties, all-terrain equipment, like this Plotmaster, is ideal.

ON A SHOESTRING
Before the costs discourage you, remember that a scaled-down version of QDM costs less. By enhancing natural habitat through forestry practices, harvesting does and restricting buck harvest, deer quality will increase. This might not be the ideal approach to QDM, but it is cer-

tainly better than doing nothing.

Also, if your property is surrounded by farmland, you might not need to invest in expensive equipment for food plots. It is often difficult to compete with surrounding farmland, so you're better off developing habitat into the best sanctuary and bedding area possible. ■

CHAPTER 4

A Grassroots Success Story

Autumn 1989 was a pivotal time in my outdoor writing career. I traveled north to Quebec's Anticosti Island and south to Texas' famed brush country to hunt whitetails. Although the Anticosti hunt was excellent, it was the Texas trip that made a lasting impression.

Anticosti offered a beautiful setting and an abundant deer herd. Unfortunately, my expectations for antlers exceeded reality. Few hunters who traveled to this fabled island were selective about antler size. In addition, the island had an extended season and a liberal two-deer either-sex limit, which meant most hunters killed two bucks. Consequently, Anticosti was not a haven for trophy whitetails. Though the hunting could be excellent, no reputable outfitter would promise you the chance to hunt a mature buck.

Texas, on the other hand, was unlike anything I had seen. The geography was much different from the heavily forested, picturesque Anticosti, but it was just as beautiful in its own way.

What especially struck me about Texas was the emphasis on deer management. I was fortunate to photograph and hunt on two of the state's better ranches, and the size of the whitetails was incredible. Both ranches emphasized producing the highest quality deer herd in numbers and antler quality.

While in Texas, I had the pleasure of spending time with Al Brothers, who many consider the father of QDM. During our time together,

Brothers explained the benefits of quality habitat, a quality herd and quality antlers. Needless to say, I received quite an education. On the plane trip home, my mind raced with what I had seen and heard.

After returning to New York, Brothers called to ask my thoughts on what I had seen in Texas. It wasn't the last time I heard from him.

HOME AND REALITY

After spending most of my life in western New York, the Texas approach to deer management was an eye opener. Although I had dreamed for years of a time when quality-racked bucks would be common near my home, such thoughts seemed far-fetched. The predominant hunting philosophy in the Northeast has always been to shoot any legal buck. Consequently, $1\frac{1}{2}$-year-olds comprise 80 percent to 90 percent of New York's buck harvest.

As my career in the outdoors gained momentum, I found myself killing small deer at home and traveling elsewhere to hunt mature bucks. In the weeks following my Texas trip, I realized it was time to reconsider how I hunted deer on my land.

During Winter 1989-'90, I decided to see if Brothers' ideas would make a difference on our

Right: This buck, killed by John Mills, inspired several landowners near Avoca, N.Y., to begin a QDM program in the 1990s.

farm. I knew our area had some of the best deer habitat in North America, but we lacked good age structure among bucks.

The big issue was determining where to begin. I knew we didn't have the magical 1,000 acres many consider necessary for managing mature bucks. Our farm is only 215 acres, but Brothers said I would see a difference in antler quality with just a few changes. First, he convinced me it was essential to protect yearlings. This was easy on our property, but knowing the wandering tendencies of 1½-year-old bucks, I doubted many would survive New York's gun season. In Fall 1990, we put yearlings off limits on our farm, much to the displeasure of those hunting with us.

However, I didn't tell my neighbors what I was doing because I didn't want to force my ideas on them. Northeasterners have a lot of pride, and they don't always take kindly to someone suggesting they do things differently. Traditions die hard, but I figured adjacent landowners would

eventually realize what we were doing, through word of mouth or by seeing better bucks.

A SAFE HAVEN

Next, Brothers urged me to come up with a plan to make resident does feel secure. He explained that if I could keep does on my property, I could also prevent some bucks from being killed. In a way, I had already started doing this. Our timber was in a forest-management plan that included selective cutting every 10 years. During Winter

Above: This aerial photo shows where the grassroots QDM program began in Steuben County, N.Y.

1989, we did a major selective cut, so everything was ready for a surge of second growth. In addition, I began planting attractive food plots in the farm's woodlots and edges.

To reduce stress on the deer population, I eliminated drive hunting in the mid-1980s. I took this low-pressure approach one step further in 1990 by only allowing stand hunting on the farm. In addition, I put a large chunk of prime bedding area off limits to gun hunting. I believed it essential for the deer to have a sanctuary, and this set-up gave them a safe place to retreat when gun-hunting pressure was at its peak.

Although I understood the importance of keeping antlerless deer in line, I also knew eliminating excess does would be difficult. For years, New York had tried to reduce the herd with deer management permits, which let hunters shoot an extra buck or doe. Despite the system's worthy goal of removing antlerless deer, not enough were being killed. Rather than shoot a doe and help the program, most hunters harvested an extra buck.

In 1993, the law changed, limiting the management permits to antlerless deer, which greatly helped the QDM movement. After the first year under this plan, the doe population dropped to desired levels and more young bucks survived.

Even before the revised permit system, the excitement of big local racks was revived when my neighbor killed a buck that grossed in the 170s. His farm borders ours, so we rushed over to see his trophy. That buck encouraged others to consider what was possible if bucks reached maturity.

Although I didn't know it at the time, two nearby landowners decided to try QDM on their farms, and they placed small bucks off limits. Their participation meant three landowners in a 3-square-mile area were practicing some form of QDM. Each of us did things differently, but our shared goal was to increase deer quality by shooting does and improving the age structure of bucks.

Initially, about 30 percent more yearling bucks survived on our property. That might seem a paltry improvement, but it was significantly better than a decade earlier when virtually no bucks survived gun season.

This estimate came from monitoring buck activity before gun season, seeing what neighboring hunters killed and observing what was around after the season. Considering the nocturnal tendencies of bucks, the 30 percent figure might have been low.

Top left: In 1989, George Jambers and Al Brothers introduced the author to QDM. **Bottom left:** In Winter 1994, the author met with several local landowners to discuss the possibility of applying QDM in Steuben County, N.Y. **Right:** Before QDM, the author usually killed yearling bucks on his New York land.

THE EXCITEMENT GROWS

As my involvement in QDM increased, I became more encouraged about our area's potential. The QDM philosophy added a new dimension to my hunts. Many locals started talking about what they saw while driving the back roads. Besides seeing spikes, forkhorns and basket 8-pointers, people began watching some trophy-class bucks.

At the end of Summer 1992, I was excited about the prospects for the upcoming deer season. Throughout the summer, three beautiful bucks — a 10-pointer and two 8-pointers —

were visiting my food plots. All three appeared to be about 120 Boone and Crockett. I watched these bucks until the end of September and then, characteristic of rutting behavior, the bachelor group broke up. I didn't see them again for several weeks.

On Thanksgiving morning, I grunted in one of the 8-pointers and shot him. The biggest of the three was killed the opening week of gun season by another QDM landowner. I never saw the third buck until after the season. I looked forward to the next season, knowing that one of the bucks had survived. My anticipation was heightened when several bucks I had never seen turned up on our property after the season. I watched the five bucks off and on the next summer. Four of them looked like 2½-year-olds. The biggest buck, an 8-pointer, was definitely older and would easily score more than 140 B&C. I figured he was the big 8-pointer from the previous year.

Despite having only three landowners with a total of 600 acres practicing QDM, the results were encouraging. I couldn't help wondering what would happen if more landowners participated.

During 1993, I hunted hard for the big 8-pointer but never saw him during daylight. Still, I shot a nice 8-pointer that ended up being the biggest buck I had taken on our property. Also, for the first time, hunters killed twice as many does as bucks in our area, further helping the adult-doe-to-antlered-buck ratio.

The QDM concept really took off after 1993. My expectations for '94 ran high as I planted food plots and prepared for the season. Several big bucks were attracted to our farm because of lush food and thick second-growth timber. One buck was a real dandy — a legitimate 150-class 10-pointer. I knew he traveled extensively because several people had seen him on surrounding farms.

The weather during the 1994 gun season was some of the worst on record, resulting in a sharp

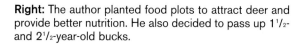

Right: The author planted food plots to attract deer and provide better nutrition. He also decided to pass up 1½- and 2½-year-old bucks.

decrease in our deer kill. Mother Nature contributed to the QDM movement by protecting a lot of bucks. On the last day of gun season, I killed a beautiful 10-pointer. Although he wasn't the slammer I had seen during the year, he was proof QDM was working.

Because many bucks survived the 1994 season, 1995 shaped up as one of the best seasons ever. Unfortunately, I ended up on the disabled list with a broken arm and couldn't bow-hunt until the first week in November. Even so, I saw some beautiful bucks. On the evening of Nov. 3, I was at full draw on a perfect 10-pointer I thought would score 140. After working a scrape, the buck walked toward my stand. At 12 paces, he stopped and turned his head to the right, exposing only his neck.

"If you'll just take one step to the right, you're mine," I thought.

It never happened. The wind shifted and he scented me. Like lightning, he wheeled on his hind legs and ran from me. On the second day of shotgun season, a QDM neighbor killed the buck as it trailed a doe through the woods. It scored 139 B&C.

I passed up several bucks during the last week of bow season and seven bucks during gun season. For the first time since we bought our farm in 1973, I didn't kill a buck on the property. I settled for a mature doe.

When the curtain closed on the '95 season, three 130-plus 10-pointers had been killed by adjacent landowners, two of whom were practicing QDM. In terms of big-buck sightings, it was our farm's most memorable season. Little did I know the best was yet to come.

From 1996 to 2001, I had more opportunities to harvest mature bucks than during the previous 25 years combined. I did not kill a buck in 2000, but I passed up more than 25. In 1997, 1998, 1999 and 2001, I killed bucks that would be trophies anywhere in North America. Ironically, the archery buck I killed on Nov. 10, 2001, was one of the bucks I had passed up in 2000. In 2000, I had had the $2^1/_2$ year-old 8-pointer in range twice in bow season and three times during the gun season.

As fate would have it, we had found his sheds and let him grow another year. When the magic moment came on Nov. 10, I was finished pass-

Left: After several years of passing up young bucks and managing the habitat, mature bucks began showing up on the author's property. **Above:** In 1997, the author killed a 140-class buck on his farm. Little did he know that things would get even better.

ing him up. Between Fall 2000 and Fall 2001, the buck had grown from a 2$^1/_2$-year-old 100- to 115-class animal to a 3$^1/_2$-year-old 140 Pope and Young trophy, making him a "shooter" in nearly any program on the continent. By practicing the Quality Deer Management Association's motto of "let 'em go, let 'em grow," my dream of harvesting a P&Y buck became a reality.

Above: In 1998, with a sound QDM program in place, the author rattled in this buck during the November rut. **Right:** In 1999, after passing up 20 different bucks, the author killed this buck during gun season. The buck was trying to breed a doe fawn that had come into estrus in the post-rut.

THE CHECKERBOARD CONCEPT

It is exciting to see what can be accomplished when landowners work together on a worthwhile endeavor.

Shortly before Christmas 1993, several neighboring landowners already practicing QDM asked me how to get more people involved. One of their ideas was to form a local QDM organization. We realized we had several obstacles, but we believed it was time to move forward. In March 1994, we presented our ideas to a packed auditorium of hunters and landowners. We generated interest and, in Summer 1994, the group elected officers and formed the Steuben County Quality Whitetail Group.

This resulted in what I call the checkerboard concept. Certainly, it is ideal to have a huge block of land managed solely for quality whitetails. However, this is wishful thinking in the East where small pieces of property are common. Not every landowner is interested in quality deer, so assembling a sizable tract of land for QDM is next to impossible.

There will always be gaps in the QDM landscape, so our area looks like a checkerboard on the map. Some properties subscribe to QDM while others don't. For example, of the 11 landowners that border our farm, only three practice QDM. Despite this, antler quality and age structure have improved — just as Al Brothers said they would.

ENCOURAGING PROGRESS

It's encouraging to see how well QDM has worked on our farm. My only regret is that I didn't start sooner. When I think of the beautiful yearling bucks I've killed over the years, I wonder what might have been if they had matured. Others involved with the Steuben County Quality Whitetail Group share this feeling.

Currently, more than 1,500 acres in my area are managed for quality deer, and Steuben County has roughly 25,000 acres in the program. With each year, more interest is generat-

Left: On the morning of Nov. 10, 2001, the author arrowed this buck as it worked a mock licking branch eight paces away. **Opposite:** After the 2001 archery season, the author figured he wouldn't have the chance to kill another trophy. However, on Dec. 9 during the gun season, he also killed this monster.

ed. One of the yearly highlights for the Steuben County Quality Whitetail Group is its annual Antler Round Up, which is held in February. In addition to an informative QDM program, official New York State Big Buck Club measurers come in to score racks from the previous season. The event is a festive affair enjoyed by all.

MINIMUM SIZES

What I find interesting about our QDM group is that nearly all participants have slightly different approaches to achieving the agreed-upon goals. For example, a "legal" buck on our farm is at least an 8-pointer with an inside spread of 16 inches. About 80 percent of the time, a buck in our region doesn't reach this size until it is 3½ years old.

When I started my QDM program, I only placed yearling bucks off limits. Then, I added an 8-point restriction, only to find it didn't work. It failed because the best yearlings and 2½-year-old bucks carry eight or more points. In effect, this restriction did not keep me from killing my best young deer. So, I raised the bar by going to an 8-point, 16-inch inside spread minimum. This has worked well, and for the most part, has protected

yearlings and 2½-year-old bucks.

I have one exception to the rules on our farm. I believe young hunters should not be strapped with minimums. Hunting a whitetail is tough enough without adding antler restrictions for new hunters. For this reason, I let my son kill any buck when he began hunting as a teen-ager. It painlessly let him learn what deer hunting is about. Now that he has a few bucks under his belt, he's passing up younger bucks. I feel certain that without letting him know what it is like to kill a whitetail buck, his enthusiasm for deer hunting would not be the same.

Some QDM participants don't make exceptions for young hunters and others have more lenient standards for spread and antler size. We try not to force everyone into the same set of rules. So far, things have worked. In spite of our differences, we are seeing improvements in antler and herd quality.

The process has been interesting, yet sometimes slower than many in the group would like. However, the crown jewel is that the program is working. And if QDM can work in Steuben County, N.Y., it can work anywhere in North America. ▪

CHAPTER 5

It's in the Stones: The Role of Soil

I was still in high school when I purchased my first Boone and Crockett record book. It cost me $15, which was a fair sum in the mid-1960s, especially for a teen-ager who made 50 cents an hour doing farm work and other odd jobs.

I bought the book because I loved to hunt and was fascinated by big game. The first time I studied the entries, I was struck by how many whitetails were killed in the farm-rich Midwest.

At the time, the No. 2 buck was killed by Roosevelt Luckey of Allegany County, N.Y., just 50 miles from my home. I remember people in the area speculating that the buck was so big because it came from the fertile Genesee River Valley.

I couldn't understand why the land in a neighboring county could be more fertile than our farmland. Of course, I was naive then and paid little attention to soil chemistry. To me, dirt was dirt no matter where it was. It wasn't until a few years later that I realized the Luckey buck's home turf was some of the most fertile land in the East. As a result, the region has produced several record-class whitetails.

SOME WILL, SOME WON'T

Some regions of the country almost never produce record-class bucks. Many factors contribute to this, including large deer populations, hunting pressure, harsh winters, lack of quality food and poor adult-doe-to-antlered-buck ratios.

Another reason, which is seldom mentioned, is the soil. In his 1933 book, *Game Management*, Aldo Leopold wrote, "There is a remarkable correlation between game supply and soil fertility throughout North America."

Leopold was a brilliant naturalist and game manager who understood long before his peers that soil is vital to the health of wildlife.

The P&Y and B&C record books indicate that regions with the richest soils generally produce the biggest bucks. The chart on the following pages — prepared by the Quality Deer Management Association — shows the number of P&Y and B&C bucks killed in the United States since 1991.

When looking at this chart, the role of soil quality in antler development is evident. For example, Vermont is steeped in hunting tradition and has long been known as a deer-hunting mecca, thanks in part to well-known hunters like Larry Benoit. Although the Granite State has produced heavy-bodied bucks over the years, it has not yielded many large racks. Limited food sources and poor soil quality are almost certainly factors. The high ratio of forested land to farmland in Vermont means the quality and quantity of food can't compare to the Midwest. Also, Vermont soils have low pH levels. Although this can be corrected by adding lime to the soil, it is not cost-effective for woodlands.

Wisconsin's Buffalo County shows what hap-

pens when things work in tandem. This region, which borders the Mississippi River and features a thriving dairy industry, is limestone country with very fertile soils. This, coupled with the region's rugged topography and a growing interest in QDM, has produced some of the biggest whitetail bucks in North America.

In the past 10 years, more than 210 P&Y bucks have come from Buffalo County. This means that a 685-square mile area has grown more record bucks in the past decade than 20 other states combined.

My home state also illustrates how good soil benefits antler growth. Western New York — from the shores of Lake Ontario to the Pennsylvania border — is excellent whitetail country. However, on average, counties within 30 miles of Lake Ontario produce bigger bucks than counties bordering Pennsylvania just 50 miles south.

The more productive area, known as the Lake Plains Region, is limestone country. On the other hand, the counties bordering Pennsylvania have a thinner layer of stony topsoil, and pH levels are substantially lower. In many cases, the soil is 100 times more acidic. Therefore, Southern Tier farms must regularly add lime and fertilizer to ensure good crop production.

Biologists know that antler beam diameter reflects a deer's physical condition. In the Lake Plains area, yearling beam diameter averages 20 millimeters or more while bucks farther south average 17 to 19 millimeters. Lake Plains yearlings also have more antler points than their cousins to the south. Although many factors can cause this, biologists pinpoint soil conditions.

ALL SOILS ARE NOT THE SAME

Whitetails can thrive in a variety of soils. For example, some areas have heavy clay while others contain rocky and loamy soils. Nearly all soil types can grow nutritional food sources, but some soils are more fertile than others. That's why some regions can grow bigger bucks than others.

Pope and Young and Boone and Crockett Record White-Tailed Deer 1991-2000

Dr. Wiley Johnson, a retired professor who taught at Alabama's Auburn University for 36 years, is a widely recognized expert on forage crop production.

"Soil is the starting point," Johnson said. "In food production, the kind of soil you have is important in determining the quality of food you can expect to grow. In a whitetail's case, soil is a foundational block for antler growth potential. The saying 'you are what you eat' is so true

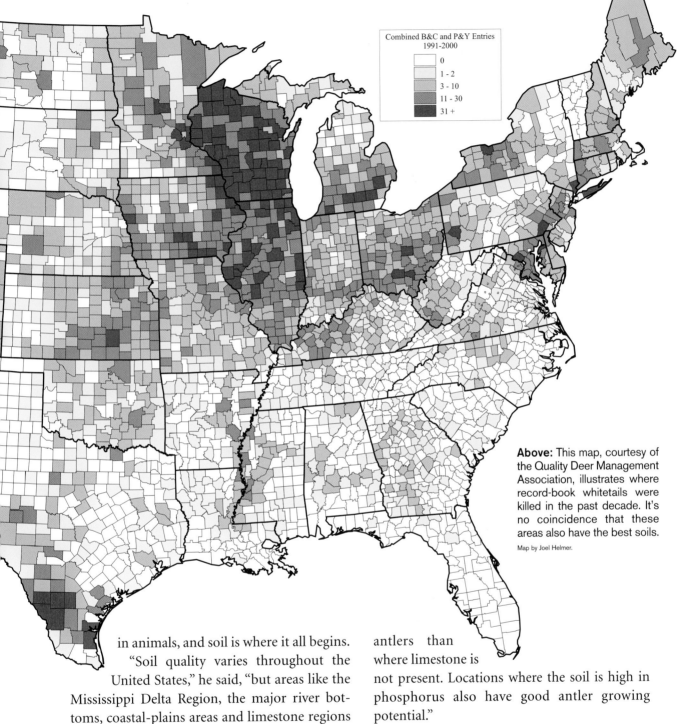

Combined B&C and P&Y Entries
1991-2000

☐ 0
☐ 1 - 2
▨ 3 - 10
▨ 11 - 30
■ 31 +

Above: This map, courtesy of the Quality Deer Management Association, illustrates where record-book whitetails were killed in the past decade. It's no coincidence that these areas also have the best soils.

Map by Joel Helmer.

in animals, and soil is where it all begins.

"Soil quality varies throughout the United States," he said, "but areas like the Mississippi Delta Region, the major river bottoms, coastal-plains areas and limestone regions offer greater agricultural potential than areas with lesser soils.

"Limestone-derived soils are high in calcium. Therefore, regions that have limestone in the soil have a greater potential to produce quality

antlers than where limestone is not present. Locations where the soil is high in phosphorus also have good antler growing potential."

Dave Buckley of West Valley, N.Y., is a retired forester and land manager. Through the years, he has helped many landowners develop their properties for wildlife. In each case, he begins by emphasizing the importance of soil.

"You can't make a silk purse out of a sow's ear," he often says when referring to people who try to grow food plots without checking pH levels.

No matter how you approach it, the foundation for QDM is "in the stones."

Water is also an important part of soil fertility. The amount of water needed depends on soil composition. Too much rainfall on permeable soils can rapidly leach nutrients required by plants. On the other hand, dry conditions can trap nutrients and prevent them from being absorbed by plants. The bottom line is that soil fertility and moisture greatly affect the quality of deer forage. It's impossible to plan for moisture, but you can get the soil ready so plant production will be maximized when it rains.

GETTING THE STONES RIGHT

Few places in North America are blessed with soils like those in the Midwest and Ohio River Valley. In fact, most areas lack so many minerals that intense measures must be taken to grow adequate food for deer.

Before you plow the first furrow, you should have a soil test completed to determine alkalinity. For less than $20, you can have a farm co-op or the county cooperative extension conduct a soil analysis and determine mineral needs. Either way, proper soil pH is necessary for productive plant growth.

Situations vary, but where I live, acidic soil is usually present where plants are stunted and the ground is covered with ferns and moss. Don't let a visual check dictate whether a soil test is necessary because failing to conduct a test is a big mistake. Landowners who bypass this step will likely waste a lot of time and money on fertilizer and seed. A soil analysis indicates how many tons of lime are needed per acre and which fertilizers are necessary and how much is required.

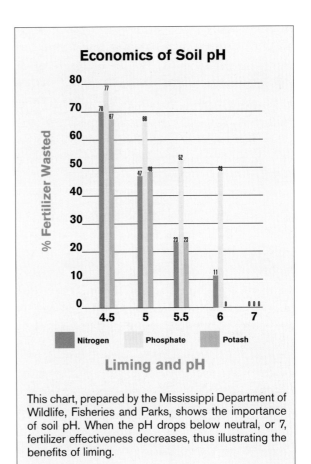

This chart, prepared by the Mississippi Department of Wildlife, Fisheries and Parks, shows the importance of soil pH. When the pH drops below neutral, or 7, fertilizer effectiveness decreases, thus illustrating the benefits of liming.

Acidity is measured on a scale of zero to 14 with a pH of 7 being neutral. Levels less than 7 are acidic.

A pH of 7 is ideal, but difficult to attain in many parts of the country where soil is sandy or rocky. If you live in such an area, strive to get the pH higher than 6, which can be done with diligent lime applications. When testing your soil, be sure you also test soil from an area you don't intend to work, such as a wooded area or fallow field. This information will help you learn about the natural food production on your property.

Don't be fooled into thinking a pH of 5.8 or 6 isn't bad because it's close to 7. Think again. Soil pH is expressed and measured on a logarithmic scale, which means that a change in one point represents a 10-fold change in acidity. For example, a pH of 6 is 10 times more acidic than a pH of 7, and a pH of 5 is 100 times more acidic than a pH of 7. This is an eye opener and a profound reason to apply lime.

Lime requirements vary widely, but a common treatment calls for 1½ tons or more per acre. Lime costs about $130 per ton when purchased in 50-pound bags. However, when bought in bulk, the cost drops to about $30 to $40 per ton.

For best results, apply half the lime before plowing and the rest after plowing. Next, add the required fertilizer and disk the soil so the lime and fertilizer are mixed into the soil. This is critical because it helps plants obtain nutrients.

FERTILIZING IS CRITICAL

Lime is the cornerstone of proper soil management, but fertilizer is the mortar. You'll find three numbers on commercial bags of fertilizer, such as 10-10-10, that refer to the pounds of nitrogen, phosphorus and potassium, respectively, per 100 pounds of fertilizer. The balance is filler.

Nitrogen is a part of all living plants and animal cells. In plants, nitrogen is a major component of protein, and it converts the sun's light into energy. Thus, nitrogen plays a critical role in determining the quantity and quality of deer food. If you increase the amount of nitrogen through multiple fertilizer applications or time-release formulas, you will increase a plant's protein content.

Nitrogen enhances antler growth. If plants are nitrogen deficient, the older leaves turn yellow, which leads to stunted growth.

Phosphorus is essential for maximum antler growth. If applied properly, it maximizes the growth and production of food plots. Phosphorous deficiency can sometimes cause stunted growth and a reddening of the stem and leaves.

Potassium, the third major component of fertilizer, helps plants create protein. Plants with adequate potassium contribute greatly to an animal's well-being. Potassium also plays a critical role in how plants use water. Potassium-deficient plants will not flourish in dry weather. Scorched leaves, weak stalks, poorly developed root systems and early leaf dropping are characteristic of potassium deficiencies.

The amount of fertilizer needed depends on many factors. For best

Left: Fertilizer inspires plant growth. One benefit of having a lab analyze your soil is that labs offer advice on fertilizing. **Opposite top:** Lime is the cornerstone of soil management. The closer your soil is to 7.0 pH, the more productive your crops will be. **Opposite bottom:** On average, it costs $250 to $600 per acre to plant a food plot.

results, consult a professional to determine how many pounds of fertilizer you need per acre for the soil type and seed you are planting.

NATURAL HABITAT SOILS

Good things happen when soil has the right amount of lime, nitrogen, phosphorus and potassium. Of course, it is not always possible to obtain optimum levels.

Although fertilizer works best when soil pH is close to neutral, many plants and trees grow well in acidic soils. Examples include oak, beech, hickory, bush honeysuckle, and blackberry and raspberry briars. Although it won't be as effective, it is often worthwhile to fertilize natural food sources.

As a general rule, I fertilize apple and oak trees by making holes around a tree's drip line with a 1-inch diameter steel bar. The number of holes depends on the tree's size. I fill each hole with one to two cups of 10-10-10 fertilizer.

CONCLUSION

A successful QDM program is made up of many parts, and they all must work together. Wise soil management is one piece of the puzzle, which is why it's important to get the stones right before moving on. ▪

Right: Food plots don't happen by themselves. It takes everything from proper layout to soil maintenance to attract whitetails like these.

CHAPTER 6

The Ultimate Food Plot

"Grow it and they will come" is a phrase often associated with food plots. The way some people use this phrase, you'd think all you have to do is till the soil and plant some seed. Unfortunately, it takes more effort than that to provide the right kind of food plot. There is a huge difference between a balanced offering of foods and the typical short-season greenfield with low-nutrition forage.

I planted my first food plot in late September 1974, shortly after my wife and I purchased our farm. With autumn rapidly approaching, I plowed a 2-acre area, dragged the soil and planted rye to attract deer to one of my favorite hunting locations. I fertilized the plot but didn't check the soil pH or add lime because of time constraints. I knew better, but I was in a hurry to beat the cold weather.

At that time, few hunters and landowners in the Northeast considered planting food plots. Our area included potato and dairy farms with lush crops everywhere, or so it seemed. Because of this, the locals who were serious deer hunters didn't bother with labor-intensive feeding programs.

When I planted my first food plot, I honestly thought I was providing our farm's whitetails with a real smorgasbord. In reality, it was nothing more than a fast-food stop because I didn't think about the whitetail's overall needs. I wanted to have an immediate food source that I could hunt. What I did was like giving a kid a candy bar instead of a nutritious, balanced meal. The rye plot certainly attracted deer, but it didn't provide balanced nutrition.

In the past 30 years, the science of managing land for whitetails has come a long way. Seeds, minerals, growth enhancers and supplemental foods are available everywhere. With the enormous amount of information and products, you'd think providing whitetails with a balanced diet would be a no-brainer. Unfortunately, because of short cuts and ignorance, all food plots are not equal — not by a long shot. Any food plot worth its weight should provide good hunting opportunities, be set up to prevent surrounding landowners from taking advantage of it, and be capable of producing great nutrition. Food plots should be 2 percent to 5 percent of your property if you want to meet nutrient requirements.

BUILD A BETTER MOUSE TRAP

After you decide to invest in food plots, you should immediately consider which plots will be used for hunting and which ones will simply be feeder plots that provide an additional food source.

In many ways, creating a food plot is like site development for a new home. A visually pleasing location might not be the right place for a plot. The biggest problems are a lack of good soil and close proximity to bordering properties. As mentioned in Chapter 5, the best soils provide the best nutrition, so the soil of each potential food plot site should be as good as possible.

Feeder Plots: Because food plots should make up 2 percent to 5 percent of your land, feeder plots are often necessary to provide the required amount of food. Of course, if enough food can be grown on hunting food plots, don't worry about feeder plots because they will compete with the plots you want to hunt over.

Generally, feeder plots are not as easy to hunt over because they are larger and more open than hunting plots. Consequently, deer use them mostly at night. When developing feeder plots, make sure they meet food requirements and are located away from neighboring properties.

Hunting Plots: If you intend to hunt over a food plot, make sure you can do so throughout the season. To get whitetails into a food plot during the day, you must provide adequate cover so the deer feel comfortable. Hunting food plots should be no more than 50 to 60 yards wide, less than an acre, and run from north to south if possible. A north-south orientation does two things: It lets hunters take advantage of western wind patterns, and it prevents excess exposure to sunlight. Plots that run

from east to west tend to become scorched because they receive too much sunlight.

Also, when looking for a potential food plot location, pay attention to how sunlight strikes the land. In most cases, the best food plots should face south, because they will get more sunlight than a north-facing plot. If your heart is set on a north-facing location, be forewarned that the plot will receive less sunlight and have cooler soils, causing plants to grow slower. In addition, the soil quality in north-facing plots tends to be poorer.

Forest Road Plots: A discussion of food plots would not be complete without mentioning how forested logging roads can be converted into food plots. For some QDM participants, this is the only possibility.

In most cases, land access trails and old logging roads are excellent spots for food plots. The key, however, is making sure enough light reaches the area. There are two ways to do this.

First, a north-south orientation is critical so adequate sunlight can reach the road. Second, the tree canopy should be trimmed on each side of the road

so light can reach the food plot. In most cases, this means cutting back the tree line at least 15 yards on both sides of the road. Although this requires a lot of work, it is worth the effort. New browse will sprout from the cut trees, and the forage yield will increase, greatly aiding the deer population. Of course, road food plots, like all feeding areas, need to be adequately limed and fertilized for maximum production.

The Setup: Sticking a food plot in the center of a mature forest usually fails because of poor soil, sunlight and drainage. It is best to place a plot along the edge of the woods and hang a stand where the prevailing wind and thermal drift are in your favor. You should also consider the angle the sun will be at when you expect to hunt. Try not to have a setup that forces you to look into the sun.

Because most deer use food plots on the fringe of daylight, stands along hunting food plots tend to be better afternoon setups. When hunting near a food plot in the morning, it's best to position the stand 75 to 100 yards from the food plot along a well-used trail that leads to a bedding area. Make sure you can enter the stand without spooking deer that might be feeding. To ensure a quiet entrance, I rake the leaves off the trail to the stand. This type of morning setup lets you ambush deer when they leave the plot en route to their daytime bedding area.

You can control how whitetails enter a feeding area by creating travel corridors between bedding areas and food plots. Use piled brush, diversion ditches or other obstructions to force deer into a predictable travel route. Enhancing food plots in this manner can significantly improve hunting opportunities.

Protecting the Resource: Work hard to avoid becoming a victim of the phrase, "I grow 'em, the neighbors shoot 'em." With more people interested in QDM, you must consider protecting younger bucks from neighboring landowners who don't

Below left: During summer, lactating does need highly nutritious food sources. **Below right:** Few forages are as attractive or as good for whitetails as clover. Place at least one exclosure in each food plot to monitor how the forage is used.

participate in QDM. If QDM is one of your goals, it's important that food plots be at least 300 yards from bordering landowners who don't practice QDM and as close to sanctuary bedding areas as possible. If this is done, bucks won't have to travel far to get to their preferred food source, and they will be less likely to be shot.

Top: After you prepare the seedbed, it's important to invest in the best lime, seed and fertilizer. **Bottom:** Roads that run through woods and brush are excellent places for food plots. For the best results, the food plot should run north/south with edge canopy cut back to let sunlight in.

GREENFIELDS – FALSE HOPE

Many sportsmen consider greenfields quality food sources and hunting magnets. In reality, a greenfield might be a good place to kill a deer, but it usually fails miserably as a good food source. As I think back to my first rye plot, I realize it could have been much better, especially if I had known more about a whitetail's needs. Rather than providing the deer on our farm with a full-course steak dinner, I gave them a one-course Spam lunch.

Another downside to that first food plot was that it was short-lived. When the snows came, the deer couldn't get to it. By the time spring arrived, the rye was in a different stage of growth and was far less attractive to deer.

In retrospect, I planted that first plot for three reasons. I had grown up on a potato farm, and after we harvested the potatoes in September, my dad would often plant rye as a winter cover crop. As soon as it came up, the whitetails on our farm hammered it. With that vision etched in my mind, I thought rye was the way to go.

A second reason was I wanted to take advantage of the rye by hunting the food source during fall. Lastly, I thought rye was an excellent food source. Rye has some nutritional value, but it took me years to figure out it doesn't adequately meet long-term needs.

FOOD PLOTS – A PANACEA

Unlike a greenfield, a true food plot provides one or more highly nutritious foods that cater to the continual needs of whitetails. With proper seed choice, it is possible to plant a food plot that offers various foods that mature at specific times.

Successful food plot development requires careful planning. Identify

Above: A hand-crank seeder lays a uniform layer of seeds.

the goals of a food plot, and keep in mind the needs of the deer herd. Nutritional requirements must be addressed for the plot to result in better antler growth and healthier does and fawns. I tell hunters their goal should be to build the best whitetail feeding and sleeping establishment they can afford. This means providing the herd with a year-round food source that is close to their main bedding area. When this is accomplished, deer, hunters and landowners all come out ahead.

THE FORMULA FOR SUCCESS

What to Plant: With so many seeds on the market, it's a wonder anyone knows what is right for their situation. After experimenting with food plots for more than 15 years, I've realized that dollar for dollar, it's tough to beat clover. Our farm and the 35-acre research enclosure on it have let me experiment extensively with different forages. For the past six years, I've had great success planting Imperial

Whitetail clover in food plots inside the enclosure and on the rest of the property. During this time, I've also experimented with a variety of other seeds, including BioLogic blends. I've learned that deer use clover plots most frequently.

With the exception of January, February and March — when New York is often buried in snow — the deer on our farm and in our enclosure feed heavily on clovers. The bottom line is clover has a summer nutritional value of 20 percent to 25 percent protein, which is the ticket for lactating does and antler-growing bucks.

Our soils cannot rival those of the Midwest, and it is difficult to get the pH above 6.5. This is one reason I plant clovers more than a crop like alfalfa, which requires better pH. However, if getting the pH above 6.5 is not a problem in your area, then by all means consider alfalfa. Alfalfa will do better in dry conditions because its roots grow deeper than clover. With a protein level exceeding 25 percent, alfalfa can turn a food plot into a nutritional mecca, not to mention a hunting magnet. Of course, a host of seeds perform as well as clover and alfalfa. Brassica has a protein level exceeding 30 percent. Mossy Oak and several other companies market brassica.

The trick in deciding what to plant depends on which seed matches the soil and region where you live. Seed companies can provide a listing of their products' compatibility with each region.

CASE STUDY

One of the most frequently asked questions I hear is, "How do you do your food plots?" After years of experimenting, I've developed a technique that works well on our property.

Where I live, spring weather is unpredictable. In some years, it seems we go from winter to summer without seeing spring. Other years, drought conditions persist throughout spring. Because of this, I typically wait until the first week in August to plant most of my food plots.

After I know the soil pH, my first step is to mow

Below: From May through June, when bucks are growing their antlers, you should offer a forage source that exceeds 20 percent protein.

the food plot location. Next, I apply the herbicide Round Up two weeks before plowing to kill grasses and weeds. Then, I lime the site if needed. After the grasses and weeds are dead, I plow, disk and float the plot so I have a good seedbed. If necessary, I end with a final application of lime.

If I'm planting clover, I broadcast a mixture of one-half winter wheat or rye seed, which are annuals, and one-half clover seed, which is a perennial, over the site. My clover seed of choice is Imperial Whitetail. However, you'll find a number of other fine clover seeds on the market.

After this, I roll the seed into the soil, which improves germination. If you are considering disking the seed in, think again. Most disking pushes the seed too deep, which prevents growth.

After the plot is planted, I pray for rain. Water is critical for seed germination. The best approach is to be a weather watcher and plant the day before a good soaking rain is expected. This will pack the seed and give it a head start on any weeds that survived the Round Up.

By the first part of September, the wheat or rye is growing rapidly, providing deer with a food source for autumn. At this time, the clover is taking hold. In March of the following year, I broadcast a thin coating of clover on top of the snow, called frost seeding, which gets into the soil through snow melt and frost.

When spring arrives, the wheat or rye and the

Protein Breakdown

It's important to consider a crop's nutritional values when planning food plots. This information from various seed companies summarizes expected crude protein values and yields.

Crop	Crude Protein	Yield Per Acre*
Alfalfa		5 to 6 tons
Bud	22-30%	
Early Flower	18-26%	
Mid Bloom	14-20%	
Winter	14-18%	
Brassica	30-35%	4 to 6 tons
Clover		3 to 5 tons
Alsike	25%	
Arrowleaf	16-22%	
Ladino	25%	
Red-Early Flower	16-22%	
Red-Late Flower	12-16%	
Corn	6-8%	1fi to 4fi tons 60 to 160 bushels
Oats	8-10%	1fi to 2 tons 80 to 100 bushels
Rye	10-14%	1 to 2/ tons 30 to 40 bushels
Soybeans	20-25%	1fi to 2 tons 45 bushels
Winter Wheat	8-12%	1 to 2/ tons 60 to 80 bushels

*Crop yields will vary by region and soil type. This data represents approximate average yields for the southern-tier region of New York.

clover begin to flourish. Around June 15, I mow the wheat or rye. What remains is a lush clover food plot that can produce about 5 tons of forage per acre for three to four years.

To further enhance the clover plots, I lightly fertilize them in spring and late summer with a 0-20-20 fertilizer. I also cut the clover to 6 to 8 inches with a bush hog or rotary mower when it is about a foot high. Depending on rainfall, I cut three to five times a summer. Farmers call this *freshening* because it keeps the protein level of the clover at its peak. However, if drought conditions prevail or if it is extremely hot, wait for rainfall before cutting. If you cut during dry weather, the clover will be further stressed and will take longer to bounce back.

To get three to four years out of clover, it is critical to spray herbicide to prevent grasses and weeds from overtaking the plot. I use POAST, which kills grasses and weeds but not clover, after spring green-up.

By planting and nurturing this way, I provide our deer with a long-lasting, highly nutritious food source for nine months of the year. If I lived outside the harsh Northern snow belt, my clover plots would be an excellent year-round food source.

In addition to Imperial Whitetail clover, I also plant BioLogic Fall Premium Perennial, which contains brassica, four different clover seeds and two varieties of chicory. I've been pleased with Fall Premium Perennial because if offers a two-

Left: As autumn arrives, bucks and does need a balance of foods. Food plots should supply a balanced, year-round food source. **Top:** BioLogic brassica grows higher than most forages, so snow must be 6 inches deep to cover it. Brassica is an excellent winter food source. **Above:** Hunting food plots should be long, narrow and less than an acre in size.

stage food plot. This means the clover and chicory offer high-quality nutrition beginning in the fall. The brassica is a taller plant that isn't preferred by Northern deer during autumn if other foods are available. However, after winter arrives, brassica provides deer with a highly nutritious food source. Though this mix is labeled a perennial, only the clover and chicory come back the next year. Brassica is an annual. I use the same planting methods for BioLogic Fall Premium Perennial as for the clover, except I don't mix annual grain with it.

Like me, the folks at North Country Whitetails use Biologic Fall Premium Perennial to sustain the deer on their New York research facility during the harsh winters. Over the years, they've found deer prefer it to anything else when the ground is covered with snow.

Whether you use a prepared seed mix or create your own, planting a combination of forages is one of the biggest keys to a successful food plot. By planting different seeds, you can make a variety of foods available at different times and provide optimum nutrition throughout the year.

MINERALS

Regardless of what you plant, it is important to provide the proper minerals and vitamins for deer to maintain strong, healthy bodies. Unfortunately, most soils are so depleted that many essential minerals are insufficient or missing. Therefore, every landowner should consider mineral supplementation.

A comparison of our research facility to the rest of our farm illustrates the need for mineral supplementation. The food plots inside our 35-acre

research enclosure are heavily limed and fertilized. In addition, the enclosure deer are fed all the natural browse they want and are given a supplemental feed that contains 17 percent to 20 percent protein and all necessary minerals and vitamins. Because of this, it doesn't matter how much mineral mix I give them — they will not touch it because their mineral requirements are already met in the food-plot forage, browse and feed mixture.

On the other hand, the free-ranging deer on the rest of our farm gravitate to mineral sites because

their habitat doesn't contain the essential minerals.

For this reason, I recommend setting up one mineral site for every 50 acres. Preferably, the sites should be near food plots. Of course, if baiting is illegal in your area, keep the mineral sites away from food plots and put them in non-hunting areas.

Research shows that calcium and phosphorus are the most important minerals for antler growth. For best results, choose a commercial mineral mix with at least a 2-to-1 calcium-to-

Above: A supplemental mineral program should be considered in any QDM program. A general guide is one mineral site for every 50 acres.

phosphorus ratio. As with seed, you'll find many great mineral supplements on the market.

By providing mineral sites, you'll offer deer a great supplement to food plots and natural browse. Let the deer decide what they need. They'll reveal their mineral requirements by how they use each site. ▪

CHAPTER 7

The Role of Good Forestry Practices

Long before I knew about QDM, I received a one-day primer on how deer use natural habitat. My instructor on that day in the late 1970s was legendary wildlife biologist, Bill Severinghaus. I was invited to tag along with him when he visited western New York to study the whitetail's effect on habitat in traditional wintering areas.

At the time, I thought deer in this area never lacked nutritious foods. However, after a day of observing heavily browsed plants, Severinghaus concluded the habitat signaled potential problems for the herd's health.

Hunters constantly ask me for advice on food plots. They want to know which foods offer the best nutrition. Their motives are genuine, but they fail to see the big picture because they don't consider the importance of good forestry practices. Sound management of natural habitat might not be exciting, but in many ways, it is more beneficial to whitetails than food plots and mineral supplements.

AFTER THE SEASON'S SUNSET

When deer season ends, most hunters leave the woods to prepare for Christmas and New Year's. Although some venture back into the woods to scout, most hunters don't revisit their hunting haunts until spring, and some don't come back until fall.

That's unfortunate. Hunters won't under-stand the status of the herd's health unless they monitor deer throughout winter.

By January, the days are getting longer, and deer search for food constantly. In Northern areas, deep snow buries farm and mast crops. In the South, mast is heavily picked over, and food plots and farm crops are in short supply.

Deer need 6 to 10 pounds of browse per day, so it's easy to understand why too many deer can quickly destroy habitat. That's why it's important to look at all aspects of habitat man-agement when formulating a QDM strategy.

THE NATURAL FOODS

Whitetails in different regions prefer different natural foods. Regardless of location, at least half of their diet comes from these foods. Therefore, addressing natural food requirements is a signif-icant part of creating a quality herd.

From a nutritional standpoint, most natural foods don't contain a lot of protein. In fact, they seldom have more than 4 percent to 9 per-cent protein.

A whitetail's diet can be made up of more than 500 natural foods, which are broken into the six categories listed below.

Forbs or weeds: Of the hundreds of forbes, very few are preferred by whitetails. Deer prefer forbes that are highly nutritious and easily digestible, and these plants are only eaten at specific times of the year.

Grasses: A whitetail consumes the most grasses during spring green-up. After summer arrives, grasses become stalky and high in fiber and lignin, and deer seldom eat them.

Mast: Mast crops, such as acorns and apples, are season specific and highly preferred by whitetails. Although low in protein (4 percent to 7 percent), mast is a great source of carbohydrates, which are needed for daily energy demands. However, mast tends to be cyclical and it is not always reliable, no matter how good a management program is.

Mushrooms: Mushrooms can be highly nutritious. Like many natural foods, their window of availability can be short. Mushrooms require a lot of moisture, so the crop might be limited during dry years.

Lichens: Lichens are a combination of fungus and algae, which grow on trees and rocks and are thought to be an excellent source of trace minerals. Although deer eat lichens year-round, Northern whitetails use them heavily during winter when food is scarce.

Browse: Of all natural foods, whitetails are most dependent on browse, which is made up of leaves and branch tips. In studies conducted at

Left: During spring leaf-out, whitetails feed heavily on any leaves within reach. **Below:** When the whitetail population exceeds a range's carrying capacity, the natural habitat quickly becomes overbrowsed. Normally, this begins with more than 25 deer per square mile.

my deer research facility, I've found that protein levels have little bearing on the types of browse whitetails prefer. For example, during leaf-out, my whitetails prefer ash, wild apple and basswood, which have protein levels of 4.8, 3.8 and 6.1, respectively. The less preferred leaves of wild black cherry, American beech and striped maple have protein levels of 13.4, 7.4 and 9.8 percent, respectively. Contrary to what some think, my studies show that deer don't choose the most nutritious leaves. Instead, deer often prefer less nutritious foods because of a combination of stimuli. The jury is still out, but most animal nutritionists I've conferred with believe deer gravitate to browse because of factors like sugar, lignin and fiber content.

The bottom line is that whitetails require a high volume of several kinds of natural foods to meet nutritional needs.

BECOMING A STEWARD

Sadly, many landowners still use a quick-fix approach to deer nutrition through supplemental feeding in winter. Feeding deer during winter is like putting a Band-Aid on a cancerous tumor. It might help in the short term, but it won't cure the problem.

At best, supplemental feeding has short-term results. Although deer appear well-nourished from corn or hay, they often aren't. In fact, supplemental foods typically do more harm than good in the long run by artificially boosting deer numbers and putting even more stress on natural habitat.

The only way to improve long-term deer health is to improve natural habitat. Soon after

spending time with Severinghaus, I devised a plan to improve the habitat on our farm. In two years, I planted rye and buckwheat food plots and 15,000 trees and shrubs.

In 1978, I decided to work on the farm's 125 wooded acres. The woods had not been logged in more than 40 years, and it showed. The forest had no understory because mature hardwoods blocked sunlight, and deer had long ago browsed away what undergrowth existed. In fact, our woods looked like a park.

Right: If a property's timber is marketable, a selective cut can be beneficial to the habitat. **Left:** When logging is complete, try to leave the tops for cover.

CHAIN SAW MANAGEMENT

I realized it would be a mistake to jump into this project without doing some research, so I contacted other landowners to find out how they managed their land. After obtaining a laundry list of advice and hearing horror stories about unethical logging, I decided to get some professional counsel from a state-licensed forester. He visited my farm and recommended I hire someone to selectively cut mature trees. The forester even marked which trees to remove.

I sought bids from several logging companies. After selecting a company, loggers removed 56,000 board feet of timber in May 1979. The cut went well, but I should have scheduled it during winter when the ground was frozen because the machines left a few scars. In addition, a winter cut would have let the deer browse the leftover treetops.

A year after the cutting, berry briars grew wherever sunlight reached the forest floor, providing abundant deer browse. Within three years, the briars were 6 to 8 feet tall, and a variety of saplings had shot up. Like the briars, the saplings provided year-round browse.

I left the treetops in the woods to speed up the regeneration process and provide more cover for wildlife. The tops also improved bedding areas and provided another nutrition source to complement food plots.

LOOKING TO THE FUTURE

Three years after the first cut, I realized the new browse wouldn't last forever.

The 1979 cut was selective, so many mature trees were untouched. I did more research and determined another cut was needed in 1989, with a follow-up cut 10 years later.

The second cut was scheduled for winter, and everything went smoothly. Combined with the first cut, the second transformed the woods from a park to a jungle, providing fantastic deer habitat.

Still, the browse wasn't enough to provide year-round nutrition. I continued to plant beneficial shrubs and food plots because I realized the land had to produce balanced nutrition for all animal life, not just deer.

In 1998, I contracted a forestry service to devise a forest manage-

Opposite: Selective fertilization of mast-producing trees can increase their production. It's best to fertilize trees around their drip-edge. **Above:** Acorns are an excellent source of energy for whitetails.

10 Steps to Better Habitat

- Improve woodlots through carefully planned timber and deer harvests.

- Consult a professional forester and explain your goals. Determine whether you are interested in creating wildlife habitat or maximizing timber production.

- With a plan in place, have the forester mark the trees to be cut. Be sure to leave enough mast-producing trees so deer have a constant food source.

- Develop a contract, and put the timber up for bid.

- If you live in the North, try to have the cutting done in winter to keep forest scarring to a minimum. Treetops should be left in the woods because they provide food and cover for wildlife and enhance forest regeneration.

- Supplement natural browse by planting shrubs and fruit and mast-producing trees in strategic locations. Be sure to protect young trees from browse damage by using tree tubes or wire cages.

- Prune fruit trees for optimum production.

- Fertilize fruit and mast-producing trees.

- Kill enough antlerless deer to minimize overbrowsing.

- Formulate a long-range plan that ensures your natural habitat produces enough food to feed deer year-round.

ment plan for the property — something I should have done when my wife and I purchased the farm in 1973.

Some landowners save money by hiring wildlife managers to devise forest plans, but I believe you should consult a professional forester. The company I hired itemized the timber, pinpointed problem areas and devised a long-range timber and wildlife management plan.

ENHANCING THE WILD

Logging is just one aspect of good forest management. Fertilization is another. Many QDM landowners use fertilizer and growth enhancers to increase the production of natural foods. As mentioned earlier, I fertilize apple trees and

select oaks to promote the growth of leaves, roots and limbs. This, in turn, leads to more browse and mast.

For optimum production, fruit trees must be pruned regularly. However, it is important not to overprune them. Don't remove more than one-third of a tree's branches. Consult a pruning guidebook, or talk to someone with experience if you have questions.

Deer habitat requires diversity, which you can provide by planting more trees and shrubs. Use commercial tree tubes to protect young trees from deer and other animals.

Although frowned upon by many landowners, herbicides can be useful. Selective herbicides affect only unwanted plant species and let

Above: With proper regeneration, natural food sources thrive and provide whitetails with the energy they need.

desirable plants flourish. If you want to eliminate problem plants or trees, be sure to consult a forester for advice. Also, check if there are regulations or restrictions on herbicides in your area.

Selective cutting in bedding areas can also improve habitat. Trees that aren't good for timber are ideal candidates. After a tree is on the ground, be sure to cut its branches so deer can reach them while browsing.

CARRYING CAPACITY

Even after providing the best habitat possible, a landowner's efforts are in vain if the deer population is not controlled, which I'll discuss in the next two chapters.

Determining the carrying capacity of a property is important to a successful QDM program. This is difficult, but if you study popular literature and learn which plant and tree species deer prefer, the process will be easier.

The following carrying-capacity estimates are from the Pennsylvania Game Commission. These estimates don't account for food plots or supplemental feeding, but they still provide a rough idea of the carrying capacities of different types of habitat.

Large clear-cuts: Clear-cutting is frowned upon by environmentalists. However, when vegetation in

Above: Use tree tubes to prevent deer from browsing on your fruit trees. **Left:** This research site in north-central Pennsylvania illustrates severe overbrowsing. Five years before the photo was taken, the area was clear cut. Foresters then enclosed five acres with high fencing so they could track forest regeneration and the effect deer have on natural habitat. The area outside the fence has no regeneration while the habitat inside the pen is lush. This site vividly shows why deer numbers must be controlled.

Browse Analysis — Steuben County, N.Y.

Since 1995, I have fed the deer in my research enclosure a variety of natural browse species daily for two reasons. First and foremost, the mixture provides a balanced diet. Second, it helps to determine which natural foods are preferred.

The accompanying list details the natural browse my deer prefer, along with two well-known

essarily gravitate to high-protein foods. If they did, striped maple would be a preferred food. My enclosure deer, as well as the free-ranging deer on our farm, won't touch it, regardless of the time of year.

Second, as the year progresses, a deer's desire for leaves decreases if more preferred foods are available. This behavior becomes evident near mid-July. By mid-August, leaf consumption nearly ceases, especially if acorns are plentiful.

Like humans, whitetails eat what smells and tastes best to them, even when the nutritional value is not as high as other foods. I've even seen deer that prefer foods the other deer in their group don't like. For example, I have a 2½-year-old buck that loves American beech browse, but the other 13 deer in the enclosure seldom touch it. I also have a 7-year-old doe that prefers aspen, while most of the enclosure deer prefer other browse. One thing is certain, though. All deer love ash, wild apple and basswood despite varying protein levels. Based on my observations, it is apparent there is more at work than nutrition, at least in terms of crude protein and fiber.

Note: The May samples were gathered in mid-May 2001 at leaf-out. The August samples were gathered in mid-August 2001 when deer stopped eating leaves. The December samples were cut in mid-December 2001. All samples came from my whitetail research facility in the Town of Avoca, Steuben County, N.Y. The first percentage in the tables represents crude protein and the second represents crude fiber.

Highly Preferred Species in Order of Preference
Percentages represent crude protein and crude fiber respectively

Species	May 15, 2001	Aug. 15, 2001	Dec. 15, 2001
1. Wild Apple	3.8% – 5.6%	11.7% – 12.3%	4.2% – 19.7%
2. Basswood	6.1% – 4.3%	6.9% – 7.4%	3.4% – 20.2%
3. Ash	4.8% – 6.7%	6.7% – 11.4%	3.3% – 30.7%
4. Aspen	9.1% – 12.9%	6.1% – 9.3%	5.1% – 17.6%
5. Hard Maple	7.0% – 8.8%	4.8% – 9.8%	4.6% – 25.7%
6. Red Oak	5.6% – 7.5%	6.8% – 11.3%	3.0% – 31.7%
7. Staghorn Sumac	6.3% – 4.1%	7.5% – 4.0%	6.0% – 28.0%
8. Raspberry plants	5.0% – 5.4%	N/A	N/A
9. Black Cherry	13.4% – 12.8%	5.9% – 7.1%	3.2% – 18.2%
10. Wild Strawberry	3.1% – 4.1%	N/A	N/A

Nonpreferred Species — Eaten If Other Browse is Unavailable

11. American Beech	7.4% – 12.7%	7.8% – 13.2%	4.3% – 23.6%
12. Striped Maple	9.8% – 8.6%	2.5% – 3.5%	2.4% – 20.4%

Highly Preferred Winter Food*

1. White Cedar	N/A	N/A	4.2% – 12.7%
2. Hemlock	N/A	N/A	3.6% – 11.2%

*White cedar and hemlock are highly preferred by my enclosure deer and by wild deer during winter. Their preference for these two types of browse at this time of the year rivals their preference for the top four preferred foods on the above list. However, white cedar and hemlock are not browsed much, if at all, during the rest of the year.

tree species they eat when nothing else is available. After we collected leaves and browse on our farm, we sent samples to the NEAS Diagnostic Laboratory at Cornell University in Ithaca, N.Y., for protein and fiber analysis.

There are two things to remember when looking at the analysis. First, after years of analyzing browsing behavior, it is apparent deer don't nec-

such cuts gets to the seedling/sapling stage, an area can support about one deer for every 14 acres, or 40 to 60 deer per square mile.

Pole Timber: Pole timber includes trees that are less than 12 inches in diameter, with most measuring 4 to 6 inches in diameter and more than 15 feet tall. Such forests are usually shady, and the trees don't produce mast. This habitat can support about one deer for every 126 acres, or five deer per square mile.

Saw Timber: Saw timber forests are a logger's dream because they have big, mast-producing trees with a high canopy. A saw-timber forest can support about one deer per 32 acres, or 20 deer per square mile. As a side note, red and white oaks produce acorns after 20 years. After age 40, the trees produce maximum yield.

Noticeable browse lines appear if there are more than 25 deer per square mile. When this occurs, the habitat and deer population start to suffer. Unfortunately, much of today's whitetail range is home to more than 50 deer per square mile. Only areas with large tracts of farmland and forests can come close to supporting those numbers, but even in such places, deer numbers are usually too high.

Agricultural crops alone cannot meet the nutritional needs of a large deer herd year-round. It takes natural habitat — made up of a variety of plant species — to provide adequate nutrition.

Deer are what they eat, so to maximize body and antler potential, you must address all aspects of habitat management. Therefore, a QDM program hinges largely on natural food sources. If you ignore natural habitat, it is impossible to have top-end results. ■

Left: When snow and cold arrive, whitetails feed heavily on hemlock, cedar and other browse. **Below:** During winter, consider cutting cull tress to provide browse.

What do you Know About Your Deer?

QDM is a puzzle with many pieces. To be successful, participants must recognize the pieces and fit them together.

One often overlooked puzzle piece is knowing and understanding the deer on your property. Too often, sportsmen pour so much effort into feeders, food plots and stand placement that they forget about the one ingredient that makes everything happen: the deer. By learning more about the whitetails on your property, you can formulate a sound plan for improving herd quality.

IN THE BEGINNING

When my wife and I purchased our farm in 1973, I had no clue people were actually managing property for bigger and healthier deer. Despite my ignorance, I ended up following some QDM principles without knowing it.

For example, from the beginning, I made it a priority to learn everything I could about the deer on our land. I did this through hours of scouting and observing whitetails throughout the year.

In the previous chapter, I mentioned that in the 1970s I followed deer biologists as they researched how whitetails used natural habitat in our area. That experience was valuable and it helped me understand the deer on our farm. The learning process was slow, but it eventually paid off.

If you hope to learn more about the deer on your land, you can't leave a stone unturned. It is not enough to know deer prefer a certain clover field, or that the oak flat on the back forty is a good place to find deer in fall. You will have a tough time outsmarting deer if you don't know where key bedding areas, transition zones and feeding areas are and how deer use them year-round.

THE POWER OF A SURVEY

To devise QDM-related hunting strategies, you must have an idea of how many deer are on your property. This is a three-step process that involves habitat, visual and technological surveys. Obviously, you will never learn exactly how many deer are on your land, but don't let that discourage you. After all, the U.S. Census is merely an educated guess.

Habitat Survey: Habitat, and especially natural food sources, reveal a lot about the whitetail population. Although not highly accurate, a natural habitat survey can give you a rough idea of how many deer you have. Look for browse lines. If they are well-defined without preferred plant species below them, you probably have too many deer.

Preferred plant species vary by region. Where I live, you'll find 40 to 50 deer per square mile when there is no regeneration of oak, ash, basswood and hard maple. When deer browse less preferred species like American beech and

88 QDM: THE BASICS AND BEYOND

striped maple, it's evident the area is overrun with whitetails.

When the population density exceeds 50 deer per square mile — even in farm country — it is nearly impossible to attain optimum antler growth.

However, a habitat survey is just the beginning of learning about the health and population dynamics of a deer herd.

Visual Survey: A visual survey can be helpful, although it has shortcomings. It is also a great way to get excited about the upcoming season.

Scouting prime food sources like clover and alfalfa fields will give you an idea of how many bucks roam your property. Early August is the perfect time for visual surveys because mast crops are still a few weeks from falling. After mast hits the ground, deer use food plots less often.

It is best to conduct summer visual surveys during the last hour of daylight when deer enter feeding areas. Whitetails typically bed all day during hot weather and are eager to fill their bellies by early evening. The only downside to summer visual surveys is that mature bucks often won't appear in fields until after dark. One way to get around this is to use a spotlight. However, if you plan to use a spotlight later in the year, check your state's regulations because some states forbid this during hunting season.

It is easiest to determine a herd's sex ratio during summer because does and fawns are

Left: By the end of July, you'll be able to judge the quality of a buck's antlers. This is a good time to learn how bucks use your property.

more identifiable. In fall, fawns lose their spots and are often mistaken for does.

Where I live, most does give birth to twins. Therefore, I know that one-third to one-half of antlerless deer are does. This helps me estimate the adult-doe-to-antlered-buck ratio. Although not exact, this method gets me in the ballpark.

Some landowners use feeders in summer to provide supplemental food and to better estimate the herd size. Feeders work, but many biologists believe they skew estimates because they attract deer from other properties.

A few summers ago, I experimented with feeders on our property from June to August. In New York, it is illegal to hunt near feeders. Although we only ran the test for three months, it was evident the deer coming to the feeders developed a welfare mentality. They stayed relatively close to the feeders, rather than dispersing and moving around the property. I definitely saw more deer, but this changed when the feeders were removed in early September and the deer returned to their routines. Overall, my experience meshed with what biologists have noted.

The ability to identify individual deer comes in handy for getting an accurate census. Deer might look the same to an untrained eye, but each deer has different facial features. You will quickly learn to tell them apart as you track them through the seasons. Daytime censuses are valuable, but it is important to conduct such surveys without spooking deer. Low-impact entrance and exit points are crucial when conducting daytime surveys. I prefer to observe deer from a distance, and I generally get the best results when watching food plots through binoculars. I stay far enough away that deer

Left: Surveys at supplemental feeders are also popular, although they tend to inflate deer numbers. **Below:** Late summer is an excellent time to conduct a property census. By checking food plots from a distance, you can estimate sex ratios and fawn survival.

never know I'm there. In addition to estimating the population, this lets me watch deer move naturally so I learn where they enter and exit food plots.

Technological Survey: Much has been written about the benefits of remote motion-sensing cameras. When coupled with habitat and visual censuses, cameras and infrared beam counters reveal things that were unobtainable just 10 years ago.

Camera surveys work best when you use one camera for every 100 acres. This lets you obtain photos of most deer on your property, and it helps determine how much of the prop-

erty deer use.

Many "photo hunters" use bait to get deer near their cameras. This might work, but be forewarned that the flash or focus noise from the camera can spook deer, particularly mature bucks.

A friend of mine remedied this by moving his cameras to the edges of fields and food plots. The strategy was immediately successful. With the cameras focused on artificial licking branches, he obtained photos of bucks in their natural activities. Bucks are less likely to be frightened by motion-sensing cameras when they are engaged in physical activity like working a licking branch. On the other hand, when they are standing at a bait pile, they tend to get startled by the flash.

To save film, position the camera three to four feet off the ground. This keeps smaller animals — like raccoons, skunks and opossums — from activating the camera. Also, keep grass and branches from the area so the camera can pick up deer in the background.

Use 200 to 400 speed print film. Although the quality is not as good as slower slide film, the exposure latitude is better.

The Trail Timer eliminates the need for film.

Right: Night cameras are a popular way to determine how many bucks roam a property. These cameras are especially useful when deer are wary and nocturnal. **Below:** When photos aren't needed, Trail Timers can monitor deer activity. The motion sensor records when deer walk past the unit.

For the past few years, I've used Model 500 Trail Timers to collect data for research on moon-related deer activity. These units record the date and time when a deer passes. They are excellent for monitoring deer activity, but some people might not like them because they don't record images.

FIND OUT WHAT THEY'RE EATING

I'm amazed how many hunters shoot a deer, field dress it and drag it from the woods without examining it. Data is a big piece in the QDM puzzle, and you can learn a lot from a harvested animal.

I always examine the stomach contents of deer killed on our property to find out what deer are eating and how far they might be traveling. Through the years, I've examined many deer with stomachs full of foods that are unavailable on our property. The most extreme case occurred about 10 years ago when a buck was shot with a belly full of corn. The closest cornfield was more than two miles away. It is possible the buck ate from an illegal bait pile, but not probable. More likely, the buck had expanded his territory during the rut to locate estrous does.

Examining stomach contents helps you determine preferred food sources in an area. Whitetails are creatures of habit, and they run together. If one deer is gorging itself on a particular food, you can bet others are doing the same. ▨

Left: Intense scouting can reveal a buck population's pecking order and show how a food plot or natural food source is being used.

Are You Shooting Enough Does?

In previous chapters, I've addressed topics vital to a successful QDM program. As significant as these issues are, they take a back seat to the importance of controlling the doe population. If does aren't kept in check, a successful QDM program is impossible.

Whenever I talk with landowners about starting QDM programs, they rarely ask how to handle the antlerless population. More than 90 percent of the time, their goal is to have more mature bucks on their properties. However, they fail to realize that killing does is a major part of QDM.

BAD CHEMISTRY

Many unpleasant things happen when the doe population is out of control. In recent years, whitetail populations have exploded throughout North America because of passive, improper deer management. For too long, hunters have overharvested bucks and underharvested does. Add the changing face of whitetail habitat and the politics of deer management, and you can see why doe herds have spiraled out of control.

When a deer population exceeds the land's carrying capacity, habitat damage from overbrowsing can be so dramatic that recovery takes years — even if all deer are removed. With too many does, the deer population and the environment are under unnatural stress. In addition, the rut is longer because there are not enough bucks to service the does. This takes a tremendous toll on bucks and results in later fawn births.

CONTROLLING THE DOE POPULATION

As legendary wildlife biologist Aldo Leopold wrote 70 years ago, "the biggest challenge in wildlife management is people management." To harvest enough does, hunters need to be part of the solution, not part of the problem. Every hunter in a QDM program must understand that does need to be harvested to meet goals.

Unfortunately, the lure of antlers often interferes with QDM goals, and some hunters make it a priority to kill the biggest buck on the property. As a result, too many hunters put off shooting does until it is too late because they believe killing a doe during the rut or early in the firearms season might ruin their chance at a big buck.

This almost always leads to failure because when a mature doe is pressured, she becomes more difficult to hunt than a buck. Why? A doe's range is usually less than 1,000 acres, and she knows every stick in the woods. Furthermore, because does usually travel in groups, multiple sets of eyes protect them from hunters.

To meet doe harvest goals, plan to shoot does early and often. It will be harder to meet your objectives if you wait until late in the season.

A RULE OF THUMB

The most difficult part of QDM is determining

how many does should be killed. It is not an easy process because things like predation, available food, winter severity and fawn mortality must be considered.

For decades, the rule of thumb for managing agricultural areas was that about 40 percent of does could be killed each year without noticing a decline in the deer population. However, this equation doesn't apply to all areas.

Drs. Grant Woods and Harry Jacobson are on the cutting edge of whitetail management in the United States. Both offer QDM consultation that emphasizes the importance of well-laid plans. For example, Woods and Jacobson urge landowners to consider factors like habitat, drought, predation, food availability and fawn survival before prescribing doe harvests.

"In places like New York's Adirondack Mountains, where predation, deep snows and climax forests exist, the deer population cannot sustain a 40 percent adult doe harvest," Woods said. "On the other hand, in vast portions of the Midwest, which are basically one big food plot, the population probably needs a doe harvest of 40 percent or more in some areas."

Jacobson agrees.

"There are no hard and fast rules for white-tailed deer management," he said. "For many areas, the 40 percent rule will work, but I've seen places where it needed to be much higher or much lower. Unfortunately, there are many places in this country where a 40 percent doe harvest is needed and hunters aren't killing half that. If you're going to err with a doe harvest, it's better to kill too many than not enough. You can bring

deer numbers back faster than you can revive damaged habitat."

Although a 40 percent harvest will get you in the ballpark, it takes on-the-ground analysis to do the job right. What works in South Carolina might not work in Illinois, Iowa or New York.

A MODEL
There is no exact formula for determining how

Above: When the adult-doe-to-antlered-buck ratio exceeds 3-to-1, many negative things occur.

many does should be killed on a property. In the previous chapter, I described how to conduct a rough deer census. After you have an estimate, you can devise a plan for harvesting does.

The following model illustrates what can happen when the doe harvest is insufficient. Note: This model is only meant to show how deer numbers can quickly multiply. It is not necessarily accurate of what will happen in the field. The model includes three assumptions about the property:

1) Deer don't enter or leave the property. In other words, they are born on the property and stay there.

2) Deer aren't killed from natural causes, pre-

Right: Does, fawns and bucks gravitate to orchards as soon as the apples start falling. Such locations are excellent places to hunt.

dation or automobiles; they are only removed by hunters.

3) Breeding does average 1.6 fawns per year. In some regions of the country the average is less than 0.5, while in others it can be 1.8 or more. I've chosen 1.6 because it is close to the average on many agricultural areas.

With these assumptions in place, let's look at what can happen. In this model, eight hunters pooled their resources and bought a 660-acre farm. The property is located in a half-forested valley and includes a mix of ridges and ravines. The farm's tillable soils have been maintained, and past crops have included corn, clover, alfalfa and grains. The farm has been open to public hunting, and in most years, pressure has been

Benefits of Aggressive Doe Harvests

- Habitat is preserved if the deer population is kept within the range's carrying capacity.

- Harvesting does will put less pressure on bucks and provide a better adult-doe-to-antlered-buck ratio.

- You will see more mature bucks.

- The number of rubs will increase.

- Scraping behavior will intensify.

- With more mature bucks, the rut will be more intense, and frenzied chasing and fighting will occur more often.

- With a balanced adult-doe-to-antlered-buck ratio, techniques like rattling and calling will be more productive.

- The rut will be more predictable. When does greatly outnumber bucks, the rut lasts up to 90 days. When the adult-doe-to-antlered-buck ratio is 3-to-1 or less, the rut will last about 40 days.

- With a more condensed rut, most fawns will be born on schedule. Fawns will develop and gain enough weight to survive harsh winters.

intense with no QDM plan in place. In short, the property's herd was hammered with hunters killing nearly every antlered buck each fall.

After buying the land, the group posted the property and started a QDM program. Although farming continued, the hunting changed significantly. The group created sanctuaries and eliminated drives and still-hunting. Stand-hunting became the primary hunting method.

The December after the property was purchased, the group made a deer census. Their count revealed 32 deer — two mature bucks, one yearling buck, 15 adult does, seven doe fawns and seven buck fawns. Therefore, the adult-doe-to-antlered-buck ratio was 5-to-1.

Despite this apparently poor ratio, the group thought 32 deer per square mile was an excellent density for building a QDM program. Their challenge was to determine how many bucks and does should be harvested to keep the population in check.

CRUNCHING THE NUMBERS

Many QDM programs begin killing does slowly. In most cases, groups want to take a wait-and-see approach. To help flatten the learning curve, the following charts show what you can expect from doe harvests of 25 percent, 40 percent and 50 percent. Remember, this is only a model, but the examples show why it's important to aggressively kill does. If a herd is not kept in check from the start, it will quickly spiral out of control.

A 25 PERCENT DOE HARVEST

In many areas, if you told hunters they needed to kill a quarter of their does, they would think you were crazy. However, as the accompanying charts show, a 25 percent doe harvest is a disaster waiting to happen in most whitetail habitats. For most regions, this number is simply too low to control annual growth.

In most areas, a 25 percent plan will quickly result in habitat destruction, widespread crop damage and a variety of stresses on all deer, not to mention other wildlife. Unfortunately, this is the kind of management being practiced throughout the United States, especially in the Northeast's agricultural regions.

If a 25 percent doe harvest were used on the model property, the deer population would go from 32 to 120 deer in four years. By that time, it

Above: Archery season is an excellent time to harvest excess does. The author killed this doe while tracking his 2001 buck.

WHITETAIL POPULATION ASSUMING 25 PERCENT OF DOES HARVESTED ANNUALLY

	START	Year 1			Year 2			Year 3			Year 4		
		PRE-SEASON POPULATION	DEER HARVESTED	POST-SEASON POPULATION	PRE-SEASON POPULATION	DEER HARVESTED	POST-SEASON POPULATION	PRE-SEASON POPULATION	DEER HARVESTED	POST-SEASON POPULATION	PRE-SEASON POPULATION	DEER HARVESTED	POST-SEASON POPULATION
Adult – Male	3	10	0	10	22	8	14	27	8	19	36	8	28
Adult – Female	15	22	6	16	28	7	21	34	9	25	42	11	31
Fawn – Male	7	12		12	13		13	17		17	21		21
Fawn – Female	7	12		12	13		13	17		17	21		21
Deer/Mile²	32	56		50	76		61	95		78	120		101

WHITETAIL POPULATION ASSUMING 40 PERCENT OF DOES HARVESTED ANNUALLY

	START	Year 1			Year 2			Year 3			Year 4		
		PRE-SEASON POPULATION	DEER HARVESTED	POST-SEASON POPULATION	PRE-SEASON POPULATION	DEER HARVESTED	POST-SEASON POPULATION	PRE-SEASON POPULATION	DEER HARVESTED	POST-SEASON POPULATION	PRE-SEASON POPULATION	DEER HARVESTED	POST-SEASON POPULATION
Adult – Male	3	10	0	10	22	8	14	25	8	17	29	8	21
Adult – Female	15	22	9	13	25	10	15	26	10	16	28	11	17
Fawn – Male	7	12		12	11		11	12		12	12		12
Fawn – Female	7	12		12	11		11	12		12	12		12
Deer/Mile²	32	56		47	69		51	75		57	81		62

WHITETAIL POPULATION ASSUMING 50 PERCENT OF DOES HARVESTED ANNUALLY

	START	Year 1			Year 2			Year 3			Year 4		
		PRE-SEASON POPULATION	DEER HARVESTED	POST-SEASON POPULATION	PRE-SEASON POPULATION	DEER HARVESTED	POST-SEASON POPULATION	PRE-SEASON POPULATION	DEER HARVESTED	POST-SEASON POPULATION	PRE-SEASON POPULATION	DEER HARVESTED	POST-SEASON POPULATION
Adult – Male	3	10	0	10	22	8	14	23	8	15	24	8	16
Adult – Female	15	22	11	11	23	12	11	20	10	10	19	10	9
Fawn – Male	7	12		12	9		9	9		9	8		8
Fawn – Female	7	12		12	9		9	9		9	8		8
Deer/Mile²	32	56		45	63		43	61		43	59		41

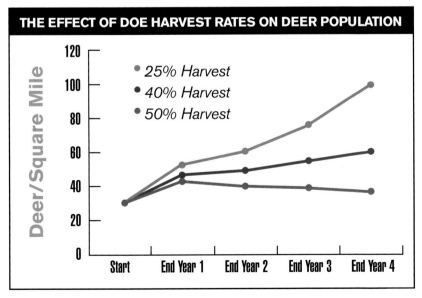

THE EFFECT OF DOE HARVEST RATES ON DEER POPULATION

- 25% Harvest
- 40% Harvest
- 50% Harvest

Above: These figures show how varying doe harvests affect overall deer densities on a model property. This is assuming no deer leave or enter the area, no predation occurs, hunters only kill adult deer, and the annual fawn survival rate is 1.6 fawns per doe. **Left:** In the model property, a 50 percent harvest might be ideal, but a 40 percent harvest would be sufficient, depending on other mortality factors.

might take decades to restore the habitat and return the herd to its proper level.

A 40 PERCENT DOE HARVEST

Forty percent is the rate preferred by many deer managers. It offers significant improvements over the 25 percent goal. If a 40 percent doe harvest is routinely achieved, the adult-doe-to-antlered-buck ratio will be near 1-to-1 in four years.

Under this program, mature bucks should be abundant and, if food sources are ample, hunting opportunities will be excellent. Also, the adult-doe-to-antlered-buck ratio will provide outstanding rut activity.

However, this scenario still falls short of keeping the property's deer population where it should be, which is about 40 to 50 deer per square mile. With 81 deer roaming the property by the fourth autumn, the habitat would experience heavy browse and/or crop damage.

Because I raise whitetails, I can attest to their prolific nature and how much they eat. When you consider one deer needs $1^1/_2$ to 2 tons of food annually, it's easy to see why habitat destruction and starvation occur when too many deer inhabit a region.

"In areas with high deer densities, you need to shoot every doe you can legally harvest," Woods once said when addressing a group of QDM landowners.

I've never forgotten his words, and as the years have passed, I realized he was right. In many areas, the antlerless harvest must be significant to keep deer herds within the land's carrying capacity.

A 50 PERCENT DOE HARVEST

Harvesting 50 percent of adult does can be a daunting task on most properties. In the case of the model property, it is essential.

If landowners meet the goal, they will have a 1-1 adult-doe-to-antlered-buck ratio by the fourth season. However, even with the increased harvest, there will still be 60 deer per square mile and the habitat will be somewhat stressed.

A 50 percent doe harvest in the fourth year means removing 10 does. Each of the eight hunters would also be permitted to kill one mature buck. If they all succeeded, the post-season deer density of 41 deer per square mile would

fall within the land's carrying capacity.

THE REAL WORLD AND BEYOND

Although the model property is interesting to study, it is far from reality. In the real world, deer die from predation, injuries and disease, and they wander over boundary lines. Even though the model doesn't account for such factors, it shows the consequences of failing to aggressively control does.

For the model, a 40 percent doe harvest is probably the best option because of the presence of predators and automobiles and because deer wander.

Above: Under traditional deer management, yearling bucks do the breeding because heavy pressure on the buck population prevents many bucks from reaching maturity.

You won't obtain your goals unless does are intensely managed. The only way to accomplish this accurately is to consult a biologist as you develop a harvest plan.

Controlling deer numbers is not rocket science. It takes knowledge, common sense and a desire for results. QDM also requires that hunters become good stewards of the land. There is joy in the journey, and the ultimate satisfaction is being part of a job well done. ▪

CHAPTER 10

Tale of the Tape: Record-Keeping Tips

I have to confess that record keeping doesn't rank high on my list of exciting QDM aspects. However, I know it's important.

Philosopher George Santanya said: "Those that cannot remember the past are condemned to repeat it," which sums up why record keeping is so important. If you neglect this step, it's hard to track your progress. Years pass, memories fade and reality becomes what you want it to be rather than what it is. After all, Barry Bonds' 73 home runs in 2001 wouldn't have meant much if someone hadn't kept track of Major League home run totals through the years.

Accurate record keeping is especially important to track reproductive performance, sex ratios, age structure, antler quality, body weight and condition, and the use and condition of forage. By monitoring and understanding these aspects, you'll stay focused and increase the likelihood of meeting your QDM goals.

REPRODUCTIVE PERFORMANCE

In most cases, you'll get a good idea of doe reproductive performance from how many does and fawns you see in late summer. I carry a pen and paper with me when scouting to note how many fawns each doe has. Then, at summer's end, I total the numbers to come up with a doe-to-fawn ratio. In Summer 2001, I saw about 100 does and 165 fawns for a doe-to-fawn ratio of 1-to-1.65. Based on state records, I know this is healthy and representative of my area.

In some areas of North America, the doe-to-fawn ratio is 1-to-0.5, which generally signifies trouble. In other areas, like the fertile Midwest, the ratio often approaches 1-to-2, indicating a very healthy herd. Because ratios vary by region, find out what state biologists consider appropriate for your area. This will give you a benchmark for evaluating your herd.

You should also note whether harvested does were lactating, which indicates reproductive performance. Does let their fawns nurse occasionally during fall even though the offspring are generally weaned by hunting season. If milk oozes from the doe's udder when you field dress her, you'll know she had fawns.

We killed eight does on our farm during 2001. Five were at least 2½ years old and lactating. The other three weren't lactating, including one yearling and two fawns.

The bottom line is that when reproductive rates drop, the herd is in trouble.

SEX RATIO

As mentioned before, knowing the herd sex ratio on your property is vital. In most areas, the objective is to have no more than three adult does per antlered buck. When that ratio is higher, a host of negative consequences occur. Habitat destruction, excessive stress on the buck population, a dull and drawn-out rut and a decline in herd health are just a few negatives of an imbalanced sex ratio.

Estimating the sex ratio in your area is a relatively

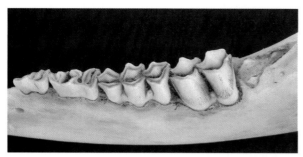

Fawn: Few hunters have difficulty aging a white-tailed fawn, whose short snout and small body are usually obvious. If in doubt, simply count the teeth in the lower jaw. If there are less than six, the deer is a fawn.

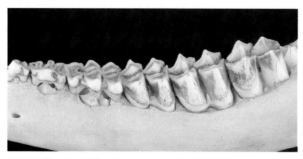

17-18 Months: The giveaway for this age is the third premolar, which has three cusps. At this age, deer also start to shed their "milk teeth." They'll either be loose or gone. Here, you can see the permanent premolars under the loosening milk teeth.

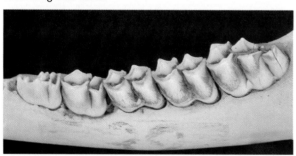

19 Months: At this age, most deer have all three permanent premolars. The new teeth look white in contrast to the older teeth. The third premolar is partially erupted.

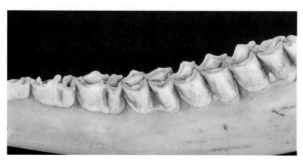

2¹/₂ Years: The lingual crests of the first molar are sharp, with the enamel rising above the narrow dentine of the crest. Crests on the first molar are as sharp as those on the second and third molar. Wear on the posterior cusp of the third molar is slight.

straightforward process. You can obtain a ballpark figure by tallying doe and buck sightings.

AGE STRUCTURE

Knowing the age structure of the deer you kill is critical. If you know the age of the bucks, you can evaluate antler size by age class. You can also determine overall herd health when comparing age to beam diameter. Larger beam diameters generally indicate healthier deer.

In addition, you should age all harvested does. Many biologists argue that you can achieve better population control by killing older, more productive does.

There are a couple of ways to determine age, but the most common method is to use the jawbone aging process. Find a biologist or someone else trained to interpret tooth wear. This method is extremely accurate up to the yearling class. Minor errors can be expected after that, but in most cases the reading will not be off by more than a year.

You can also extract an incisor tooth and send it to a lab for testing. This method is the most accurate, but it is more expensive than tooth-wear aging. Expect to pay about $20 per test. For this reason, tooth-wear aging is usually the best option.

Aging deer on the hoof can often turn into a guessing game. However, with experience, it is possible to accurately estimate buck ages. The book *Aging and Judging Trophy Whitetails* by Dr. James C. Kroll is an excellent resource that should be a part of every QDM library.

ANTLER QUALITY

Antler quality is one of the easiest ways to evaluate herd health. State biologists have long known that many variables affect antler beam diameter, so make sure you keep detailed records of beam diameters from the bucks you kill.

Take the beam diameter reading one inch above the burr, or base, of the main beam. I recommend investing in a good pair of calipers so measurements can be taken to the millimeter. If you don't have calipers, at least take the readings with a quarter-inch tape measure.

A state deer biologist can provide normal beam diameter for different age classes in your area. If the bucks you kill tend to be smaller than normal for your region, something is probably wrong with the deer herd and/or habitat. The problem often stems from too many deer, a poor sex ratio and poor or insufficient food. Recording beam diameters will reveal whether your efforts actually result in a quality deer population.

In addition, I encourage QDM participants to score the bucks they kill with the Boone and Crockett system. B&C scoring sheets record a host of information such as inside spread, beam length, point length and antler circumference. Make sure these records are easily retrievable. Note that the Pope and Young system is based on B&C scoring.

BODY WEIGHTS AND CONDITION

In addition to antler data, body weight is a key indicator of herd health. I have hunted a great deal with Saskatchewan outfitter Bentley Brown, and he advocates recording live and dressed weights of every deer killed. Everyone involved in QDM should follow his approach.

As with antler size, you should look for trends in buck and doe weight. If weights are below normal, it is usually from the same problems that cause smaller antlers.

When recording this data, make sure you keep track of when the deer was killed because bucks can lose up to 25 percent of body weight during the rut. In western New York, the average pre-rut buck live weights are: yearlings, 130 to 140 pounds; 2½-year-olds, 150 to 175 pounds; 3½-year-olds, 180 to 215 pounds; and 4½-year-olds, 190 to 250 pounds.

It might be surprising, but it is important to record the weight of doe fawns because body weight determines whether a fawn can reproduce. In my area, biologists believe a high percentage of doe fawns will be bred at 6 to 8 months old, assuming they weigh 85 to 90 pounds by the end of November.

Obviously, the average doe fawn weight is a

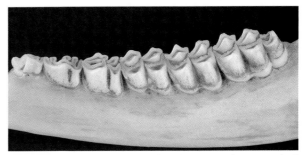

3½ Years: The lingual crests (inside, next to the tongue) of the first molar are blunted, and the dentine of this tooth's crest is as wide or wider than the enamel. The dentine on the second molar is not wider than the enamel.

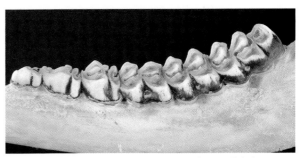

4½ to 5½ Years: It's often hard to distinguish between these two ages. The lingual crests of the first molar are almost worn away. The posterior cusp of the third molar is worn at the cusp's edge so the biting surface slopes downward. Wear has spread to the second molars.

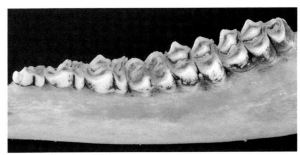

6½ to 8½ Years: By 6½, wear is moderate on the first premolar and heavy on the second and third. Little or no enamel remains on the first premolar. At 7½ and 8½, the first molar might be worn within 2 or 3 mm of the gum on the outside and 4 or 5 mm on lingual side.

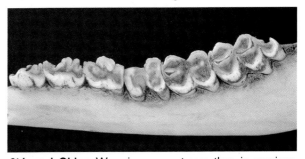

9½ and Older: Wear is more extreme than in previous photo. Pulp cavity might be exposed in some teeth. Some teeth worn to the gum line.

gauge of herd health. In addition, knowing the average weight of doe fawns will help you evaluate rutting activity in December and January (in the North), which is when fawns are bred.

In general, a deer's overall appearance can reveal whether parasites or other problems are affecting the herd.

CONDITION AND USE OF FORAGE

Finally, it is important to keep track of the condition and use of forage on your property. Do this by placing wire exclosures in all food plots. Generally, a 4-

Above: By tallying the number of does and fawns you see during late summer and early autumn, you'll get an idea of the does' reproductive performance. **Bottom right:** In addition to hunting logs, it's also a good idea to keep track of interesting deer behavior. **Bottom left:** Accurate records keep a program focused and moving forward.

foot high, 3-foot wide exclosure is sufficient. Exclosures are inexpensive and reveal how heavily deer are using a food source.

It is also a good idea to make one or two exclosures around a small portion of wild habitat. These exclosures should cover at least 15 square feet, and the wire should be high enough to prevent deer from getting inside. Normally, a 6-foot high exclosure will keep deer out.

CONCLUSION

Collecting data is certainly not the most exciting aspect of QDM, but it should be considered an integral part of every program. Record keeping lets QDM participants monitor their progress and evaluate whether the program is affecting the deer herd. ∎

Boone and Crockett Scoring

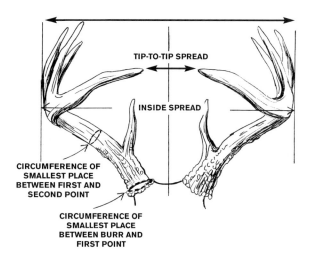

TIP-TO-TIP SPREAD

INSIDE SPREAD

CIRCUMFERENCE OF
SMALLEST PLACE
BETWEEN FIRST AND
SECOND POINT

CIRCUMFERENCE OF
SMALLEST PLACE
BETWEEN BURR AND
FIRST POINT

Above: This illustration shows some of the measuring points used for Boone and Crockett scoring. For an official scoring sheet, visit www.boone-crockett.org.

CHAPTER 11

From Buttons to B&C:
Is it Possible?

eer hunters everywhere are fascinated with QDM. Wherever I go, people want to talk about it. If you heard their questions, you'd think there's a magical formula for producing record-class bucks.

I'm amazed at how many people think big bucks can be raised from a bag of minerals or clover seed. I'm equally amazed by how often I hear hunters say age is all it takes to grow a Boone and Crockett buck. In reality, getting a button buck to B&C category is a journey that includes many variables.

As a teen-ager, I believed age and quality food were the magical ingredients needed to produce a 170-class buck, the B&C minimum. As time passed, my thoughts changed. I realized that even if we knew the equation for growing a B&C buck, it wouldn't guarantee a B&C rack.

Since building my whitetail research facility in 1995, I've had the pleasure of working with some of the most knowledgeable whitetail experts in North America in hopes of learning more about a buck's growth potential. Their insights and the results from our studies are enlightening.

WHAT IT TAKES

Age, genetics, habitat and herd management are the four basic ingredients needed to produce a 170-inch buck.

Despite an explosion of knowledge, many hunters still wonder why their areas don't produce trophy bucks. In reality, the environment required to produce many B&C bucks doesn't exist — at least not in the wild. Even if an area provides the four ingredients, those components must align flawlessly to produce several record-class whitetails. Even perfect conditions don't guarantee B&C bucks.

Let's look at two scenarios — the real world and a controlled environment — to see how various factors affect antler growth.

The real world is any place in North America with wild whitetails. These deer must cope with everything nature and humans throw at them. The stress heaped on them often reaches absurd levels, resulting in suppressed antler growth. I believe stress on wild deer is cumulative, and antler growth is suppressed in varying degrees depending on how much stress is placed on a herd.

ENVIRONMENT

Whitetails deal with environmental stress even when human activity is eliminated. For example, in remote Southern areas, extreme heat and parasites heavily burden deer. In Northern climates, whitetails deal with a far different problem: brutal winters with deep snow and cold temperatures. Winter stress can severely suppress antler growth, especially when in conjunction with overbrowsing.

No matter where it occurs, drought is a major suppressant of antler growth, especially during the critical antler-growing season of April through July. Bucks need large quantities of lush, nutritious food to reach their antler potential.

Insects are another environmental stress. Insect swarms have killed domestic animals as well as deer.

FOOD

Most deer need 1^1/$_2$ to 2 tons of food per year for optimum health. For the best antler growth, it is critical to keep nutritional composition high at all times. Therefore, during the antler-growing season, food sources must be high in protein and provide essential vitamins and minerals. During the rest of the year, food sources need to be high in carbohydrates to provide proper energy.

For the best antler growth, habitat must support the wildlife. Bucks can grow impressive antlers when they receive a variety of highly nutritious foods. However, these foods disappear quickly when too many deer live on a property. Therefore, bucks living on overpopulated range won't always grow the racks they are capable of. This is why it is important to keep the deer population within the range's carrying capacity.

Unfortunately, the answer isn't as simple as planting farm crops and food plots. For example, soil is often overlooked. As I discussed in Chapter 5, it is no coincidence that some of the biggest bucks come from regions with fertile soil. For example, the Midwest's Grain Belt

contains some of the most productive soil in North America. Therefore, it's easy to understand why the region has produced more than 65 percent of B&C bucks.

POPULATION

Deer density is as important as food when it comes to maximum antler potential because antler growth suffers when density is too high.

Brothers Dave and Rick Griffith operate a

Above: The journey from a buck's first to fifth set of antlers is filled with tribulations. Even with great genetics, it's seldom possible for a buck to reach Boone and Crockett proportions. The buck on the left is 1½ years old and the one on the right is 5½.

state-of-the-art whitetail gene/semen collection operation in Huntingdon, Pa. After years of observing antler growth in their breeder bucks, the Griffiths have reached some interesting conclusions.

"Whitetails are very sensitive to overpopulation and do poorly if there are too many deer," Dave said. "We've found that if we leave a breeder buck with a group of does from breeding time to fawning time, the buck's antlers are

almost always smaller the next year. When we remove the buck from the does right after the breeding is over, antler growth doesn't suffer. Bucks — especially top-end bucks — do better

when they can be alone or in bachelor groups.

"We know that if bucks are forced to be around too many deer, they'll seldom reach their full antler potential."

ADULT-DOE-TO-ANTLERED-BUCK RATIO

It doesn't take much for herd sex ratio to significantly suppress antler growth. For example, antler growth suffers in areas with an adult-doe-to-antlered-buck ratio of more than 3-to-1. When herds exceed this ratio, the rut becomes too long, especially for mature bucks. A 2-1 ratio isn't bad, but for maximum growth, the ratio should be 1-to-1.

The rut lasts about 45 days in areas with balanced ratios. However, when the adult-doe-to-antlered-buck ratio exceeds 3-to-1, the rut can last 90 days or more. This is dangerous because in the North, it means the rut stretches into winter. Rutting bucks enter winter so worn down they can't recover before their antlers begin growing in April. In such instances, it's not uncommon for mature bucks to die from the added stress of winter.

Tom Morgan, a deer breeder from Union City, Pa., has studied how stress affects deer herds.

"Everyone knows the rut drives a white-tailed buck crazy, and it doesn't matter if the buck is behind a high fence or roaming in the wild," Morgan said. "We've discovered that if you let a buck breed more than 10 does there is a high probability that his body cannot recover before he begins to grow another set of antlers. And, if he's physically behind in April, his

antlers will be smaller than the previous year."

Dave Griffith agrees.

"Allowing a buck access to too many does is not the way to go if maximum antler growth is your goal. A buck cannot control himself during the rut, and too many does will drain a buck of everything he has in him," he said. "When a doe comes into estrus, she takes a buck on a two- to three-day ride he can't control. Because he doesn't know when enough is enough, he gets himself into all kinds of trouble — often trouble he can't recover from."

THE RUT

If that isn't enough, bucks receive more stress from rival competition during the rut. If you add this to the list of things bucks endure throughout

Left: White-tailed bucks like this one that score more than 200 Boone and Crockett points are one in a million. To produce top B&C bucks, it takes incredible soil, genetics, food and management. Few places in North America have this combination. **Right:** Balanced, highly nutritious food is critical for antler and body development.

the year, it is easy to understand why wild bucks usually don't reach their antler potential.

On good range, bucks are rolling in fat when the rut's seeking phase begins. However, in the two weeks before full-blown breeding, bucks move constantly in search of estrous does. This nonstop dash to ensure survival involves everything from chasing to fighting to rubbing and scraping. Clearly, bucks expend a lot of energy during the rut, and they often do so without eating, thus increasing the strain on their bodies.

PREDATION

Predation also affects antler growth. Dogs, coyotes, wolves and humans kill hundreds of thousands of deer each year. However, noncontact predation is also a powerful factor. Several projects conducted by Dr. Aaron Moen of Cornell University have indicated that the mere presence of predators can result in underdeveloped antlers.

In one project, Moen studied how snowmobiles affect the heart rates of captive deer. He also studied the heart rates of fawns in response to wolf howls.

The average heart rate of a white-tailed deer varies. A bedded deer has a rate of about 72 beats per minute. Other rates include standing, 86 beats per minute; walking, 102 beats per minute; and running, 155 beats per minute.

In the fawn study, Moen found that wolf howls increased a fawn's heart rate to as much as 265 beats per minute. In the snowmobile study, heart rates were as high as 209 beats per minute.

Although undocumented, hunting pressure certainly has a similar effect. Stress on deer can be great in areas with long seasons and a lot of hunters.

An increased heart rate increases metabolism, which depletes fat reserves. Any form of predation places some stress on whitetails, which can negatively affect deer from a physical standpoint and prevent them from reaching their growth potential.

LESSONS BEHIND FENCES

By reducing stress, you can improve the odds of watching a buck fawn grow into a B&C-class whitetail.

Some people argue that it's impossible to reduce stress. However, today's technology makes it possible to create environments where stress can be controlled.

Many deer breeders have experimented and

Below: When the rut explodes, competition among bucks becomes fierce. The stress of fighting can be significant, and injuries can cause suppressed antler growth the following year.

A Real-World Example

Understanding what it takes to raise whitetails in various environments is complex and often misunderstood. These four photos show what can happen when good food, average genetics and age combine.

This buck was born in the wild on our farm in Spring 1995. During Summer 1995, we built a 35-acre research enclosure. Despite going to great pains to eliminate trapping wild deer, this buck, which was a fawn at the time, managed to elude us when we drove the wild deer out. After getting permission to keep the buck, time took over. With the enclosure's great feed and low deer population, the buck thrived.

As a yearling, the buck had a beautiful 7-point rack, and by age 2, the rack measured 122 B&C. By the time the buck was 3 years old, its antlers scored more than 150 B&C. At age 4, the buck we named Spook scored 168 B&C.

Unfortunately, in December of his fourth year, Spook was involved in a fight with another mature buck and died after breaking his neck. Who knows what his antlers would have looked like from ages 5 to 7, when bucks generally grow their biggest racks. However, this buck, born in the wild on our farm, is a testimony to what can happen when age and nutrition blend. And, this is further proof of what QDM brings to the table.

1.5 YEARS OLD

2.5 YEARS OLD

3.5 YEARS OLD

4.5 YEARS OLD

END NOTE

Because this buck shows what can happen in the "real world," the four images offer guidance for setting up QDM harvest guidelines. As mentioned earlier, one of the first steps in QDM is to protect yearling bucks. However, the importance of protecting $2^{1}/_{2}$-year-old bucks is seldom mentioned.

In most cases, bucks experience a significant jump in antler growth every year from ages $1^{1}/_{2}$ to $4^{1}/_{2}$. However, the increase between ages $2^{1}/_{2}$ and $3^{1}/_{2}$ and then $3^{1}/_{2}$ and $4^{1}/_{2}$ is most impressive. As you can see, Spook grew from a 120- to a 150-class buck between ages $2^{1}/_{2}$ and $3^{1}/_{2}$. Because of this, most QDM participants strive to ensure bucks are protected until they are $3^{1}/_{2}$.

---

discovered what it takes to raise trophy bucks. Of course, their work is done behind high fences where deer are in relatively stress-free conditions. To produce big-racked bucks, most breeders become students of genetics and meticulously study deer for desirable characteristics.

"After genetics, I look at a host of factors that I have to build on to get full antler potential," Morgan said. "I see habitat as critical. If a buck's environment is not right, it doesn't matter what kind of genetics he has. He will not reach his full potential. So this means controlling and improving everything from natural settings to a balanced diet to eliminating the number of other deer he can interact with to prohibiting dogs near the buck.

"I've been in this game long enough to know that if I can't provide a top breeder buck with the best conditions, I can't expect him to grow the kind of antlers I think he's capable of," Morgan said.

The Griffith brothers use a similar approach. They use elaborate breeding and handling facilities to keep their top-end bucks calm and comfortable. By catering to a buck's every need and eliminating stress, the Griffiths produce record-class whitetails.

"To reach optimum antler growth, every white-tailed buck needs to go into a new antler-growing season with a full tank, so to speak," Dave Griffith said. "Think of it this way — a whitetail's bone marrow system is like a fuel tank. If its bone marrow and body condition are not in top condition when the sun says 'Start growing antlers!' they can't possibly reach their antler potential. So, body mainte-

nance is critical when it comes to antler growth. Removing stress helps achieve the results we're looking for."

REALISTIC EXPECTATIONS

Although Morgan and the Griffiths grow their huge bucks in controlled environments, there is no question we can learn much from these deer. Knowing their potential puts many things in perspective.

For example, when analyzing regions for antler potential, I look at how an area relates to the six stress factors. If all six affect an area, top-end potential probably won't exist. However, if only two factors affect a region, I want to hunt there because I know it probably holds big bucks.

That is not to say I'm a trophy hunter. In fact, I believe many hunters put too much emphasis on the magical score of 170.

It's unrealistic for hunters to think they stand a chance of killing a buck that big in the wild. I have hunted whitetails for more than 35 years, and only twice have I killed a buck that grossed more than 170 inches B&C. A 170-class wild buck is truly a freak of nature.

When hunters ask what kind of bucks they can expect to see in places like western Canada and Texas, I tell them not to base their goals on what they read in maga-

Above: During the rut, a buck's range balloons to 4,000 or more acres as it searches for estrous does. This causes stress, which can hamper antler growth. **Right:** When you consider the stress of the rut plus the stress of winter, it's amazing any buck can grow a larger rack the following year.

zines or see on television. Be realistic, and try to find out what an average buck is. I believe a realistic expectation in the best deer habitat in North America is 140- to 150-B&C. Considering the stress that affects deer, it's hard to find 150-inch bucks in the wild. In many places, few, if any, exist.

In fact, research states that the 140- and 150-inch bucks in Saskatchewan, Wisconsin and New York could easily be 160- to 170-inch bucks if they lived in controlled environments. Furthermore, most deer researchers say heavy stress, whether it comes from drought, predators, severe winters or other environmental factors, can suppress antler growth by 20 percent or more.

CONCLUSION

It takes more than meets the eye to transform a button buck to a B&C trophy. In fact, for most North American bucks, it is nearly impossible.

In the future, hunters will probably kill huge bucks that rival those killed by Milo Hanson and James Jordan. These awesome bucks are a part of the mystery of life, just like 7-foot-tall basketball players and home-run hitters like Hank Aaron, Mark McGwire and Babe Ruth. However, is it realistic to think the road from buttons to B&C is a given? Not hardly. For the most part, 140 to 150 inches is as good as it gets in the best fair-chase environments.

Stress comes in myriad forms, and one thing is certain: It hurts the hat size of every wild buck. ▪

Right: Although this isn't a Boone and Crockett buck, the author believes the buck is realistic for most of North America. The rack scores about 150 B&C.

The Whitetail's Spring

Nature has no hard and fast rules for when one season ends and another begins. Instead, the changing seasons are a gradual process, especially in the North. Most people associate spring with wildflowers and cute, spotted fawns. However, in the northernmost reaches of the whitetail's range you won't see such sights until late May.

Deer are gaunt by the time winter breaks. Fortunately, this is only temporary. Because of increased daylight, whitetails shed their winter coats. Where population densities are high, it's not uncommon to see the ground dotted with hair. Whitetails are extremely social, and they often groom each other, which removes loose hair.

Lengthening daylight also triggers increased appetites, and bucks and does gravitate to any greenery they can find. In early spring, finding green shoots of grass can be difficult. As a result, aggressive behavior often occurs when bucks, does and fawns compete for food. By the time green-up is in full swing, deer can be seen feeding during the day in lush areas.

GROWING THE BONE

In the North, white-tailed bucks begin growing antlers in early April. As antlers grow, they are encased in a network of blood vessels and skin tissue called velvet, which nourishes the antlers. At first, antler growth is slow, with only an inch or two of growth by the end of April. But by May, antler development kicks into high gear. The growth rate accelerates dramatically with the increase of daylight hours. Peak growth occurs from mid-June to late July when the days are longest.

Bucks move less and become secretive when their antlers are growing. Their hormonal level is at its lowest, so they are not aggressive. As a result, bucks form bachelor groups during spring and summer. By being passive and avoiding conflict, bucks seldom damage their velvet antlers.

Although the rut is months away, some bucks display limited rutting behavior during spring. Mature bucks exhibit their dominance by pulling their ears back aggressively when around other bucks. They will also occasionally fight other bucks with their front hoofs.

Throughout the year, bucks also visit old scrapes and leave their scent by working overhanging licking branches. This behavior isn't as common in spring as it is in fall, but nonetheless it can occur frequently, especially when the old scrape is along a heavily used trail.

FAWNING TIME

When leaves begin to bud in the North, fawning time is near. A whitetail doe has a lot to deal with at this time. She's heavy with fawns and must deal with the harsh task of driving off her fawns from the previous year. This is essential for a healthy herd. By forcing her buck fawn to leave her and

Right: By April, nearly every buck has shed its antlers. If stress is low and nutrition high, some bucks can carry their antlers into late March and early April. **Left:** When young, fawns nurse several times a day. **Above:** At birth, a fawn is about the size of a loaf of bread and weighs between 6 and 9 pounds.

the area, she prevents inbreeding.

The whitetail's fawning season is like frosting on spring's cake. After a gestation period of 200 days, most Northern fawns are born in late May or early June. Because they are born at the end of spring when warm days and nights are common, fawns avoid the unpredictable weather of early spring. This gives them a better chance at survival.

Does give birth to two fawns under the right conditions. Generally, one fawn is a buck and one is a doe. Each fawn weighs 6 to 9 pounds, and its body is about the size of a loaf of bread. To say fawns are vulnerable at this stage is an understatement. Their survival depends on the doe, and many factors determine whether they will make it through the first week of life.

THE CRITICAL FIRST WEEK

It's critical that fawns are born where they can hide from predators. After giving birth, the doe

eats the afterbirth, cleans the area and bathes her fawns to eliminate scent, which prevents predators from locating the fawns. Usually, a fawn can walk a short distance within a half-hour of birth and several hundred yards after an hour. To stay a step ahead of predators, the doe moves the fawns shortly after birth and constantly relocates them during the first few weeks. Also, to increase the chances of survival, does force their twins to bed apart and feed them only two or three times a day. A doe seldom beds with the newborns. Instead, she stays just out of range in case predators approach. If this happens, she springs into action and comes to the fawns' rescue.

THE EDUCATION PROCESS

Although a doe attempts to keep her fawns apart, it can sometimes be quite a chore to make sure it happens. Fawns imprint easily and are extremely social, so they tend to want to be with their mother or sibling. Years ago, I realized that a whitetail behaves like a human. Fawns, like children, are often strong-willed and don't always heed instruction. On several occasions, I've photographed does attempting to bed fawns apart, only to have the fawns try to get closer to each other after the doe leaves. It can be rather humorous to watch, especially when the doe uses discipline.

Seeing a doe communicate with her fawns is a special experience. When a doe seeks a fawn at feeding time, she approaches the bedding area uttering mews and low grunts. When the fawn hears its mother's call, it rises from bed and often prances to the doe's side before locking on to her nipples and drinking up to 8 ounces of nourishing milk. The feeding takes less than a minute. When nursing, the fawn's tail wags excitedly as the doe grooms it. After nursing is complete, the doe might continue to groom the fawn before walking off with her offspring in tow.

To instill nature's harshness in her offspring, a doe won't excessively pamper her fawns. She'll shower them with affection, but she'll also be a strong disciplinarian. A doe picks her fawns' bed-

ding sites, decides when to feed them, and determines what they should be subjected to. When they disobey her, she physically disciplines them.

If a fox or coyote gets too close to a fawn within the first few weeks, a doe will charge the predator or try to lead it away from the fawn's bed. Also, if a doe hears her fawn bleating, she'll come to rescue it. I've seen how well a doe uses her front hoofs to defend herself and her offspring, and it's nothing I'd want to mess with.

Does tend to rule the woods when fawns are vulnerable. Seldom will a doe let another deer get close to her fawn during its first month. On several occasions, I've seen a curious yearling buck approach a fawn, and the doe has always

Left: By spring green-up, bucks and does frequently feed in fields throughout the day. **Right:** Fawns are curious and sometimes overly adventurous. This fawn was bedded in a clover field before it got up to check out a buck that was feeding nearby.

been quick to let him know she was in charge. Does can be so aggressive at this time that most bucks simply shy away from them.

By the time the summer solstice arrives on June 21, most fawns are large enough to outrun most of their enemies. The fawns begin bedding and traveling with the doe wherever she goes. Although it will still nurse, a fawn begins fending for itself as summer arrives and the next phase of its life begins. ■

CHAPTER 13

The Whitetail's Summer

Songwriter George Gershwin wrote, "Summertime, and the livin' is easy," and nothing better describes a whitetail's life during summer. It's a fairly uneventful season for deer. Typically, bucks eat, grow antlers and hang out in bachelor groups, while does teach their fawns the ways of the wild.

SUMMER'S DOE/FAWN BOND

Summer for a whitetail fawn is like grade school for children. At this time, a doe is a mother, provider, protector and teacher to her offspring. She is busy, especially if she has two or more fawns.

During June and July, fawns grow by leaps and bounds and command as much of a doe's time as she can spare. From birth to about 10 days old, fawns spend nearly 90 percent of their time bedded in thick cover. About the only time they move is when the doe returns from her nearby lookout for grooming and feeding.

On average, fawns are fed three to four times per day for 10 to 30 minutes before the doe forces them back to their beds. A doe generally beds 100 to 150 yards from her fawns where she can stay alert to danger.

Although does might move their fawns a long way, most limit their home range to about 20 acres. In New York, the Department of Environmental Conservation has run a radio telemetry study for several years. The results show that does commonly confine their movement to areas no larger than 10 acres for extended periods of time.

During summer, it is important for a doe to select a home area with nutritious food, which is critical for her and her fawns' health. Because of this, summer food sources should have protein levels of 10 percent to 20 percent. In large forested areas where this is not possible, fawns tend to be smaller than farm country deer, especially if the population is beyond the range's carrying capacity.

Sibling fawns bed separately until they are about 1 month old. A fawn's weight increases from 6 to 8 pounds at birth to 25 to 30 pounds by the end of its first month, enabling it to outrun most predators. Also, by the time a fawn is 1 month old, it starts to eat vegetation.

Fawns become more visible after 2 months as they travel and feed with their mothers. Fawns are full of life at this point and often run and frolic.

Fawns born in late May and early June can weigh 40 to 50 pounds by August. By September, they feed more on forages and become less dependent on their mothers' milk. Although they might continue to nurse throughout autumn, fawns can be weaned by the time they are 10 weeks old.

Throughout its first two months, a fawn's social contacts are limited to its sibling and mother. As summer progresses, fawns begin to interact with their older sisters, who are included in their mother's social group. It's not uncommon for fawns to curiously approach bucks. When photographing fawns in feeding areas, I'm always amazed by how

little fear fawns have for bucks. Does usually run from bucks, but fawns will curiously approach a feeding buck. On more than one occasion, I've laughed as a fawn tried to touch a buck's antlers or search for a place to nurse. Seldom have I seen a buck get aggressive or irritated by a fawn. The buck will just paw at the fawn gently or walk away.

GROWING THE BONE

Like does and fawns, bucks gravitate to protein-rich food during summer. Because of the nutrients needed to grow antlers, bucks feed heavily on nourishing foods. In farm country, soybeans, clover and alfalfa, which are more than 20 percent protein, are preferred. Bucks often feed several times a day and can consume more than 15 pounds of highly nutritious food within 24 hours.

By June, a buck's antler growth rate is at its peak. Unlike April and May, when antler growth is minimal, the long days of June and July bring tremendous growth. Some antlers grow a quarter inch or more per day.

By the end of July, the days grow shorter. Diminished daylight causes antler growth to slow, and by the first week in August the process is complete. After this, it takes about three weeks for the antlers to mineralize. Most Northern bucks then shed their velvet from the end of August to the first 10 days of September.

In 120 days, bucks grow between 120 and 200 inches of bone, which would be like humans growing two arms every year.

Summer doesn't technically end until the end of September, but I've always considered the velvet-peeling period to be the end of the season. In the North, bucks begin peeling around Sept. 1. After raising whitetails for more than 15 years, I believe each buck has a genetic code that determines when it sheds velvet. Every buck I've raised has peeled its velvet at nearly the same time every year.

Some bucks might take two to three days to complete the process, while others might take less than an hour. I've long believed that the time it

takes to peel is determined by a combination of factors including air temperature, insect density and the buck's tolerance to the smell of blood. Next to a knock-down, drag-out fight during the rut, the peeling process is the most energy draining behavior for whitetails. If a buck peels his velvet within two hours, he will be totally exhausted when finished.

SUMMER SOCIAL BEHAVIOR IN BUCKS

Bucks and does remain segregated during sum-

Below: Throughout summer, bucks bed most of the day. At this time, the stress caused by insects can be immense. **Lower left:** Bachelor group behavior is common during summers when bucks bed and feed together.

mer. For the most part, they are only close to each other when feeding, and even then, they usually stay separate.

Home Range: During summer, bucks are secretive and move less than during the other seasons. A buck's range in summer often depends on water, bedding areas and food availability. In some fertile agricultural areas of the Northeast, bucks cover little more than 500 acres during summer. In more remote regions, their range might be 1,000 acres or more. However, this is still significantly less than the average 4,000 acres bucks cover during autumn.

Hierarchy: As summer progresses, it's common to see bachelor groups. These groups form a dominance order — primarily through aggressive behavior displays — long before autumn's hard-antler season arrives. Yearling and mature bucks tend to form their own bachelor groups, although mature bachelor groups occasionally tolerate some yearlings. I've seen bucks establish their pecking order by boxing, chasing, shadowing and vocalizing aggressively. Even though they can be aggressive, bucks remain protective of their velvet-covered antlers.

Scent Marking and Rutting Behavior: Throughout the summer, bucks exhibit a moderate level of scent-marking and rutting behaviors. Flehmening, or lip-curling, occurs throughout the year — even though it's primarily associated with breeding. Lip-curling lets a buck trap scent from a doe's urine in his nose so he can determine whether the doe is approaching estrus. In the summer, this behavior is probably a conditioned response.

A buck also works a scrape's licking branch sporadically during summer. Scientists believe bucks leave their scent on the overhanging branch to communicate identity and dominance. When working a licking branch, a buck deposits scent from his nasal, forehead and preorbital glands. Bucks seldom paw the ground under a licking branch during summer like they do in autumn when they aggressively work scrapes.

September's cooler, shorter days signal an end to the whitetail's slumber time. By the end of September, bachelor groups begin breaking up, red summer coats change to autumn brown, and fawns lose their spots. It's time for October and the rigors of the breeding season. ■

Opposite top: Unlike does, fawns often feed and interact with bucks during summer. **Opposite bottom:** It's not uncommon for bucks to exhibit rutting behavior during summer. Here, a yearling buck tries to push a mature buck. **Above:** By the end of August, a buck's antlers are finished growing and the velvet starts to peel.

CHAPTER 14

The Whitetail's Autumn

By late September and early October, the nights are cool, and the apples and mast have started falling from the trees. It's the grandest time of the year for whitetails, but it's also a time of great change.

As September eases into October, a decreasing photoperiod prompts whitetails to grow a thick winter coat. This heavier coat, coupled with warm weather, means whitetails are less active during the day. It's common for bucks and does to bed 70 percent of the time. During early fall, bucks usually stay separate from does and seldom venture out of their core areas. Does stay in family groups and continue their normal patterns. As a result, you'll see more does than bucks in September and October.

FOLLOW THE FOOD

Food dictates deer movement in early autumn. Whitetail bucks commonly lose up to 25 percent of their weight by the end of the breeding season, so they spend September and October building fat reserves. During summer, whitetails crave high-protein foods, but by fall, high-energy foods like corn, acorns and beechnuts make up a larger portion of their diet. Consequently, during autumn, whitetails gravitate to cornfields, apple orchards and mast-producing forests.

After raising whitetails, I know they eat a lot during September and October. If the right food is available, bucks and does will eat more than 12 pounds of food per day. With activity low and food intake high, whitetails gain considerable weight from the end of August through October.

TRANSITION TIME

By September, bucks begin reacting to increased testosterone. This natural sex drug triggers scraping, antler rubbing, sparring with bachelor group members and lip-curling whenever they find doe urine. Bucks also become more vocal.

Scraping Behavior: In the past 20 years, I've studied and photographed hundreds of bucks making scrapes, and every year I become more intrigued. Like rubs, scrapes are key signposts, and it's not unusual for several bucks to work the same scrape if it is in a highly used area.

When making a scrape, a buck deposits as much scent as possible by rubbing his preorbital and forehead glands and salivating on the overhanging licking branch. He will also paw away debris beneath the licking branch and urinate on the exposed earth.

After years of observations, I've noticed that Northern bucks usually splay their legs when urinating if the scrape is made before the end of October. After this, they'll rub-urinate, placing their hind legs together and urinating through the tarsal glands. By rubbing the glands together and urinating through them, bucks leave behind more scent.

Rubbing Behavior: As the rut inches closer to

its November peak, white-tailed bucks increase their rubbing activity to leave scent and make other bucks aware of their presence. No tree is safe because mature bucks rub big and small trees. Though I've photographed yearlings making rubs on trees larger than 4 inches in diameter, most of their rubbing is done on trees less than 2 inches in diameter.

When a buck rubs his antlers on a tree, he also rubs his nose and forehead gland, and will likely lick the rub to leave his distinct odor. Though other bucks can relate rub size to animal size, it's the odor that lets other bucks know who's been there. In my experience, this odor is as important as rub size in determining a buck's social status. Also, researchers believe the scent, or pheromones, deposited on rubs are a priming function that helps determine when breeding begins.

Sparring and Fighting Behavior: Dominance fights intrigue all whitetail enthusiasts. While their antlers are growing, some bucks try to intimidate other bucks by fighting with their hoofs. After velvet is shed, the bucks begin sorting out who's boss by shadowing or sparring. When shadowing, a buck pulls his ears back and stands his hair on end. While doing this, the dominant buck often snort-wheezes. Usually, shadowing and vocalizing are enough to make an inferior buck back down.

I've photographed and observed many sparring matches between bucks. Technically, sparring is not fighting, but more like a friendly wrestling match. The two participants merely push and shove each other. Sometimes these matches last a half-hour or more, although most are brief. Hoof fighting, shadowing and sparring let bucks sort out a hierarchy. However, if these activities don't work, bucks resort to drastic measures.

When two bucks of equal size compete for does, it's possible they will fight to the death. In all my years of pursuing whitetails, I've only seen a handful of such fights. They seldom last more than five minutes, and the action is fast and furious. It's an unforgettable experience, and the amount of noise generated is incredible. Often one, or both, of the combatants sustains serious injuries from the flurry of flashing antler tines. As with shadowing, bucks often use vocalizations during fights, addressing one another with snort-wheezes or aggressive grunts.

Left: As autumn progresses, bucks become more active, and scraping behavior intensifies. **Opposite:** By the time the leaves have fallen, bucks actively pursue all does in their area to find one ready to breed. By trapping scent from a doe's urine in its nose and Flehmening, or lip-curling, a buck can tell if a doe is in estrus.

DOE BEHAVIOR

Compared to bucks, autumn is rather subdued for does. Aside from how they react to testosterone-driven bucks, their lives aren't much different than other times of the year.

Doe family groups keep together during fall, bedding a great deal and making every attempt to steer clear of bucks. Does know how dangerous antlers are, so they avoid contact with bucks. A doe that is not ready to breed will flee for her life.

Except for shifting food sources, a doe and her family group live in a relatively small area. The doe group's home range is seldom more than 1,000 acres. Despite being weaned in August, fawns nurse throughout the fall, although nursing frequency is far less than during summer.

THE RUT

The peak of the rut varies throughout the United States, but the behavior associated with it is the same. By the end of October, a Northern buck's rutting switch is thrown. The days are short and cool, and a few does are coming into estrus, which sets the stage for the rut. The rut can be divided into three phases: seeking, chasing and breeding. All three phases share similar behavior, but each is slightly different.

The Seeking Phase: The arrival of November marks a transition in whitetail behavior. As if on cue, a buck's range increases. It's not uncommon for a buck to cover 4,000 acres or more at this time.

About two weeks before full-blown breeding, the rut's seeking phase begins. In a fine-tuned herd, where the adult-doe-to-antlered-buck ratio is less than 3-to-1, buck sightings will be frequent. Bucks bed very little during this time as they move from one doe group to another in search of estrous does.

When a buck comes upon a doe group during the seeking phase, he'll often move from bed to bed, carefully smelling and lip-curling before moving on. Bucks rarely frantically chase does at this stage. Of all the times to hunt, this part of the rut might be the best because a buck's movement through funnels and along scrape and rub lines is more predictable. Unfortunately, the seeking phase quickly blends into the chase phase.

Opposite top: By November, chaos arrives in the North. No doe is safe when bucks begin the chase phase of the rut. **Opposite bottom:** When two mature bucks overlap each other's territory, or are in pursuit of the same doe, a serious fight often ensues. These fights seldom last longer than five minutes, and usually end when one buck runs away or is seriously injured.

The Chase Phase: The chase phase often gets confused with the seeking phase because the two periods overlap. This second phase usually begins a week or so before full-blown breeding. Like the seeking phase, the intensity of the chase phase depends on the adult-doe-to-antlered-buck ratio. It can be spectacular if there are enough mature bucks.

During the chase phase, does are close to estrus, and bucks are frantically trying to locate them. At this point, a buck will chase every doe he encounters. Such meetings often resemble a horse trying to cut a calf out of a herd. Bucks are persistent, knowing they will eventually find a doe that won't run.

A buck's vocalization when pursuing a doe can

Opposite: Only large, mature bucks rub trees this large. A buck leaves as much scent as possible by rubbing his nasal and forehead glands on the rub. **Above:** During autumn, does and fawns stay together and spend much of the day resting or feeding.

be very loud and aggressive. I've often heard bucks grunt loudly while chasing a doe, which sometimes sounds like a drawn-out moan.

During the chase phase, scraping and rubbing continue, which can be intense, especially in a well-tuned herd. The chase phase often includes intense fights, especially when two bucks pursue the same doe.

The Breeding Phase: This stage is the essence of the rut. Because of many factors, the breeding period varies by geographical region. In the

North, the peak of this phase can range from the first week in November to the end of the month. The length of the breeding phase depends largely on the adult-doe-to-antlered-buck ratio.

When a doe finally enters estrus, she accepts a buck's company wherever she goes. In many parts of North America, the adult-doe-to-antlered-buck ratio is so heavily tilted toward females that any buck can easily find a hot doe. When breeding begins, scraping nearly ceases and bucks curtail much of the activity of the seeking and chasing phases.

Rather than traveling, a buck stays with an estrous doe for up to 72 hours. For the first 24 hours, the doe smells right but isn't ready to breed. During the second 24 hours, the doe is in full estrus and will let the buck breed her several times. Because she still smells right for the final 24 hours, the buck remains with her.

During those three days, the buck moves only when the doe moves. Because most does cover little ground, deer activity seems to halt during the breeding phase. Only when a doe cycles out of estrus does the buck look for another hot doe.

The first does to come into estrus often cause a commotion by attracting several bucks. When that happens, a dominant breeder will try to run off all

intruding bucks to stay in position to breed the doe. When a buck that is tending an estrous or near-estrous doe encounters other bucks, he'll snort-wheeze or use a tending grunt to intimidate the competition.

Post-Rut Recovery Time: Because they have no time to rest or eat, dominant breeder bucks can lose 25 percent or more of their weight during the rut. By the time the prime breeding period ends, a buck's testosterone level starts to plummet. Dominant bucks are so worn out that they often don't survive a hard winter. In regions with high adult-doe-to-antlered-buck ratios, the stress

Above: Does flee from aggressive bucks throughout the seeking and chasing phases of the rut. However, when the does enter estrus, they stand and wait for the buck to breed them.

of an extended breeding season substantially decreases a buck's chance at survival.

With less testosterone to drive them, bucks rest and feed as soon as breeding ceases. With the wonders of autumn behind them, whitetails prepare for winter by spending December feeding on whatever food sources they can find. ▪

The Whitetail's Winter

Winter is the most stressful time of the year for deer, especially in the North. As a native Northerner who has lived in farm country for more than 50 years, I can attest that these conditions are harsh. Winters are seldom pleasant, and many are downright brutal. Some years it seems no whitetail could survive the cold and deep snow. Somehow, though, most deer figure out a way to make it to spring. Every time I think about what whitetails go through, I'm in awe of their resilience and ability to survive.

WINTER RANGE

In remote areas like New York's Adirondack Mountains or Maine's famed Allagash region, whitetails migrate to their familiar wintering areas when heavy snow begins falling in December.

I've seen several deer migrations in the Adirondacks, and each time it impresses me. This migratory behavior, which scientists refer to as yarding, has been passed from generation to generation, and without it, deer couldn't survive harsh wilderness conditions.

Whitetails travel from five to 30 miles between their autumn and winter ranges. They generally yard in thick conifer swamps, thereby conserving energy and gaining protection from predators. Dense swamps are more wind resistant than open hardwoods, which shelters deer from wind chill.

Winter in farm country is a different story. The only movement that resembles a migration is when whitetails abandon north-facing areas for south-facing locations. This usually requires little more than a two- or three-mile shift.

HIBERNATION ON THE HOOF

In most Northern regions, winter is worst during the short days of December and January. This causes some distinct biological shifts for whitetails. With less daylight and lower testosterone levels, bucks become less aggressive. Factors like nutrition, health and range condition — combined with decreased testosterone — determine when bucks drop their antlers.

Casting, or shedding, generally takes place from December to March. Popular literature suggests that older, more mature bucks drop their antlers first, and I've found this to be true where rut-worn bucks inhabit an area with marginal food sources. However, in locations with abundant food, I've seen trophy bucks keep their antlers until late February. I'm also convinced that genetics greatly influences when each buck drops its antlers. The bucks I've raised drop their antlers on nearly the same day each year when they are in good health and not overly stressed.

Another biological shift occurs as whitetails adjust to winter. During early winter, a deer's metabolism decreases. Therefore, deer require

148 QDM: THE BASICS AND BEYOND

less food for survival. By midwinter, deer slow down even further, and they appear to be hibernating. Scientists refer to this as semihibernation, which makes deer resistant to nutritional deprivation and winter stress. During this stage, whitetails eat 30 percent less food, regardless of food availability, and reduce overall activity by up to 50 percent.

THE FOOD FACTOR

The downside to this semihibernation state is that whitetails are reluctant to move to find food. I often see this when I go into wintering areas to cut browse. During hard winters, I've cut trees within 300 yards of bedding areas just to get the deer interested in a new cache of food. Other times, I've seen whitetails less than half a mile from good browse but uninterested in looking for it. It seems food has to be under their noses for them to show interest. This complicates matters because whitetails need at least 6 pounds of browse a day during winter. If they don't move to look for food, their physical condition deteriorates quickly.

Snowfall also affects how actively deer look for food. I've noticed that deer move freely as long as the snow is less than 1½ feet deep. When the snow is deeper than 2½ feet, deer activity diminishes significantly.

If whitetails spend winter in poor habitat,

Left: When heavy snows arrive, bedding becomes the primary winter behavior for whitetails. In some areas, whitetails bed more than 90 percent of the time.

Above: During winter, whitetails need 5 to 7 pounds of browse per day. Therefore, it is critical they have enough good, natural habitat.

they deteriorate rapidly. For this reason, it's important that deer winter where there is nutritious food. In the Northeast, deer prefer browse like ash, apple, sumac, hemlock, red maple, basswood and white cedar. When whitetails begin feeding on other foods like American beech or striped maple, it's an indication preferred foods are no longer available.

Though whitetails are sluggish during winter, they can be aggressive when food becomes scarce. While photographing, I've often seen deer fight each other for food or browse. Such displays are memorable, especially when a doe competes with her fawns. Winter is a time of survival of the fittest. In the deer world, it's every deer for itself — if you want to eat you have to fight for it.

REST – THE KEY TO WINTER SURVIVAL

What's the most common whitetail behavior? It might surprise some, but it's bedding. The average whitetail beds a whopping 70 percent of the day. In the North, it's not uncommon for whitetails to bed more than 90 percent of the time during winter.

More than 25 years ago, Cornell University researcher Dr. Aaron Moen documented that a whitetail's heart beats 72 times per minute when bedded, 86 times per minute when standing, 102 times per minute when walking, and more than 155 times per minute when running. So, in the dead of winter, whitetails can conserve a lot of energy because they spend so much time resting.

During snowstorms, whitetails usually stay bedded until the weather subsides. During this time, they get up only to stretch and relieve themselves. Only after the storm passes do they attempt to find food. I've often seen deer remain in an area the size of a football field for days when conditions were poor.

Generally, winter activity is limited to the middle of the day, although whitetails become more active if the temperatures warm. When deer move, bucks and does often socialize with other deer around them. Does groom their fawns. Bucks, having reformed their bachelor

groups, groom, rub and spar (if they still have antlers), and occasionally work overhanging licking branches.

Sparring matches can be humorous if one or both bucks have lost their antlers. When photographing in an Adirondack deeryard, I once observed a big-bodied buck that had shed its antlers attempt to spar with a medium-sized 10-pointer. The buck without antlers gingerly

Right: Limited breeding occurs in December and January if doe fawns mature or in areas with poor adult-doe-to-antlered-buck ratios. **Below:** Bucks often spar in winter. This nonaggressive behavior is common with enough mature bucks in the population.

tried to place his forehead between the burrs of the other buck's antlers. It was like watching a tugboat push a barge around. He had the right idea but didn't have the equipment. I've also watched antlerless bucks attempt to rub trees.

When a warm-up ends and the cold returns, the fun and games are over, and deer revert to more dormant behavior.

THE PREDATOR'S ROLE

The predator's role in managing whitetail numbers is controversial, especially when it comes to winter stress. Popular literature states that coyotes do not significantly affect whitetails. However, some of the best biologists are reconsidering this.

Coyotes and wolves are opportunistic and are arguably the best hunters on the continent. Coyotes definitely affect our farm-country winter deer herd, but nothing like in remote regions where snow depth is significant.

A Cornell University study illustrates how predator stress can negatively affect whitetails. In 1978, Dr. Moen was involved in a project to determine a whitetail fawn's heart rate in response to recorded wolf howls. The results illustrate how quickly a whitetail can go from sleeping or resting, which Moen called idling, to full alert. In one test, a bedded fawn's heart rate went from 100 beats per minute to 198 beats per minute just 14 seconds into the wolf howl. The fawn jumped to its feet, and the next readable heart rate, taken four seconds later, was 297 beats per minute.

Increased heart rate burns more energy — energy a deer might not have. Because of this, stress can negatively affect an animal's physical condition. A wolf or coyote doesn't have to chase a deer to stress it.

Stress, whether it stems from severe cold, deep snow, lack of food, human encroachment or predation, affects all deer in a herd. By the end of winter, the cumulative effect of stress often hurts whitetails. However, winter gives way to spring. The cycle is complete, and once again the whitetail looks forward to warmer, sunnier days. ■

Above: If the snow isn't too deep, deer will attempt to feed in food plots. **Right:** When a buck's testosterone level drops, he sheds his antlers.

Hunting Strategies That Make QDM Shine

To make sure you don't compromise your QDM goals, you must examine the effects of traditional hunting methods. Deer can travel several hundred yards after being spooked, so they often end up fleeing to another property. To prevent this, eliminate drives and still-hunting, which tend to pressure the herd.

LOW-IMPACT HUNTING

Whitetails are more active during the day if they feel safe, so it is necessary to eliminate or curtail human activity. Take extra care to avoid detection, and practice low-impact hunting, which puts the least amount of pressure on a herd while letting you meet harvest goals.

Whitetails might not think and reason as we do, but don't underestimate their memories. Through the years, I've seen incredible examples of how deer learn by experience. As a result, I believe deer go out of their way to avoid places where they have encountered danger.

This is why it is important to avoid hunting prime bedding areas. You should also examine your hunting approach around feeding areas — especially during firearms season.

TRANSITION ZONE HUNTING

Low-impact hunting often confines you to transition zones, which deer use to travel between bedding and feeding areas. Transition zones vary in length from 50 yards to a half-mile and are often located in saddles, tight funnels, diversion ditches, stream crossings and thin strips of woods.

Such areas are usually full of sign like rubs, scrapes and well-used trails. They are also where bucks and does are the most vulnerable and easiest to hunt. In addition, deer often travel by themselves, which lets you kill select deer without spooking and pressuring other animals. Transition-zone hunting is also the best way to keep whitetails on your property.

For a QDM program to thrive, use hunting strategies designed for transition zones.

HUNTING THE PRE-RUT

In the North, the pre-rut begins after bucks shed their velvet and lasts until about Oct. 20. For the most part, it is a time of leisure for whitetails. Deer eat more, and are therefore more predictable. Because of this, I confine pre-rut hunting to areas near food sources. In late July and early August, I begin scouting for areas with abundant corn, clover, acorns, apples, alfalfa and beechnuts.

When scouting during the pre-rut, I look for well-worn trails near food sources. I also try to determine how far deer travel from their bedding areas, and I keep scouting sessions low-key and nonthreatening by scouting during late morning and midday when deer are bedded.

I look for trees where I can place a stand at

least 15 feet high no more than 15 yards downwind of the trail. In addition, I try to find a tree that will break up my outline, because nothing is worse than looking like a lollipop in the sky. If a tree doesn't offer natural concealment, I hang evergreen boughs behind me.

Teasing Tactics: Although rattling and grunting are generally considered rut strategies, I use both during the pre-rut because bucks often spar during early fall. I gently tickle my rattling antlers together at medium volume. My sparring sequences last less than five minutes, and I repeat them every hour if necessary. This technique tends to be most productive during the first two hours and the last two hours of the day.

During the pre-rut, I limit my calling to short, medium-toned grunts and doe bleats, which are good locator calls. If I see a buck walking through the woods, I'll grunt to stop him. If he's interested, he'll stop after one to three grunts and come my way. If a buck starts toward you, stop calling before he spots you.

A doe bleat is useful when action is slow and you are trying to attract an out-of-sight buck. Generally, I'll give two or three bleats and repeat the process every 30 to 45 minutes if nothing responds.

Beating a Buck's Nose: Always make sure your stand is downwind of where you expect to shoot. It if isn't, move to a different location. Nothing can destroy a hunt faster than having the wind work against you. You can fool a whitetail many ways, but you can't fool its nose. Generally, there is more moisture in the morning than the afternoon, so scent lingers longer in the morning.

I prefer a slight breeze over calm conditions. If your stand is properly placed, a light, steady breeze will carry scent downwind and away from where you expect a buck to show up. Without wind, your scent will ride thermals, which are drafts caused as the ground heats and cools.

Hunting in hilly country can be challenging because uneven terrain causes the wind to constantly change direction. However, on calm days, you can hunt hilly country effectively if you remember these basics: In the morning, as the ground warms, air rises and thermals blow uphill. Later in the day, as the ground cools, the wind reverses and blows downhill.

If the wind is not in your favor, try scent elim-

Right: In a QDM program, low-impact hunting strategies are a must. If your setup is right, techniques like rattling and calling work well.

inators. By spraying scent eliminator on your clothing and wiping it over your neck and face, you'll remove a lot of odor.

However, if you don't control your breath odor, everything else could be in vain. Breath odors spook deer as quickly as any other foreign smell. An average person exhales 250 liters of air every hour, and emits a lot of odor in the process.

Chlorophyll tablets, which can be purchased in most drug stores, are one way to control your breath. Or, take an apple and suck on a piece as you sit in your stand. Only do this if there are

Above: Mock licking branches are one of the author's key hunting strategies. During Fall 2001, he killed two does and a Pope-and-Young buck as they worked a mock licking branch 15 yards from his tree stand.

apple trees nearby, otherwise you'll cover one foreign odor with another.

HUNTING THE RUT

By late October, a buck's desire shifts from food to sex. If you're ready for this change, you'll be in position to kill the buck of your dreams.

Bucks rub, scrape and chase, but does create the rut. Therefore, my hunting strategy revolves around pursuing bucks as they interact with does.

By late October in the North, the whitetail's rutting hammer is cocked and ready to be tripped. After eight years of exhaustive research with Vermont wildlife biologist Wayne Laroche, I've concluded that the timing of the seeking, chasing and breeding phases varies from year to year.

After monitoring more than 75 does for eight years, I've concluded that the second full moon after the autumnal equinox marks the start of the North's seeking phase. In a fine-tuned deer herd, nearly all bucks are consumed with breeding does after this full moon. Consequently, bucks let their guard down and become vulnerable at this point.

Nearly all of my rut phase hunting is in transition zones. If conditions and habitat are right, several trails will pass through such areas. The best hunting site is usually near the trail with the most rubbing and scraping sign in mid-October. If sign is spread throughout the transition zone, you must take several steps to make one trail more attractive than the others.

How to Make a Whitetail Superhighway: To make a trail more attractive, I hang two to five mock licking branches over the trail, spacing them about 50 yards apart. Using plastic draw ties, I attach a mock licking branch to an existing branch about five feet off the ground. If there is no existing branch over the trail, I attach the mock licking branch to a wire strung between trees. I expose the earth below each licking branch, which makes the site look like a natural, active scrape. I've used attractant lures on the branches, but have discov-

Top Right: The author has been successful ambushing bucks as they work scrapes in transition areas, such as funnels and travel corridors. **Bottom Right:** A buck works a mock licking branch.

ered they're not necessary.

Bucks usually use the mock scrapes within 48 hours. The mock scrape will concentrate deer activity, so be sure to clear a shooting lane that is at least 10 feet wide.

In November 2001, I shot a beautiful Pope and Young buck and two does using this tactic. In each case, the deer came down the scrape line and worked the mock licking branch. You might be surprised to hear that does work licking branches, but in my experience, nearly all deer work a mock licking branch as they walk past it, providing you with a clean shot at close range. This is an incredibly effective strategy that I discovered years ago while photographing deer, and it is ideal for QDM hunting.

Calling Tactics for the Rut: My strategy for grunt-

Below: Rattling can be effective – especially if you know big bucks are in the area. The two-week period before the breeding phase of the rut is the best time to rattle in a buck. **Right:** Using decoys can be exciting. For best results, add motion to your decoy.

ing during the rut is similar to my pre-rut calling, but I include the buck's tending grunt, which can be an excellent buck stopper if used properly.

Often, when a buck is with a hot doe and is frustrated by her rejections or interrupted by another buck, he will grunt with a ticking cadence. This unique vocalization is generally used around an estrous doe, so it usually elicits a positive response from bucks.

If I'm hunting in thick cover and a buck walks through, I'll use a tending grunt to bring him within range. This is a great call to use when bucks are on the move and the rut is boiling over.

Rattling: During the rut, bucks are aggressive, which makes rattling a great strategy. I rattle forcefully for about five minutes, because real fights seldom last longer. Rattle for a minute and a half, pause for 30 seconds, and repeat this two more times. Once again, remember that rattling is most effective during the first and last hours of the day. However, don't rule out midday, especially during November's full moon period. I've rattled in some nice bucks during midday at this time of the year.

HUNTING THE POST-RUT

I am an opportunist when it comes to hunting the post-rut. Although does breed during this time, deer behavior is different, which requires special tactics. After the rut, I hunt food sources close to prime bedding areas. By concentrating on feeding areas, you'll get close to surviving bucks and doe groups. All deer, but particularly bucks, need to gain and maintain body weight to survive winter, so everything is secondary at this time — even sex.

Smart scouting is extremely important for killing post-rut nocturnal bucks. A bedding area's relation to food and water can't be emphasized enough because it reveals how a buck moves to and from

the bedding area. During the post-rut, find bedding areas close to feeding areas. Bucks are weary and don't want to travel far for food. As a result, you'll often find them bedding in thick cover within 200 yards of mast or standing field crops.

If you find a trail leading to or from a bedding area, look closely at the tracks. If most of the tracks head toward the feeding area, the trail is probably used in the evening. If the tracks head into the bedding area, the trail is used in the morning. If you know a whitetail's escape routes, you can plan strategies and determine stand locations.

To ambush a post-rut buck, you need to be as inconspicuous as possible. This means limiting how much time you spend in the area you plan to hunt. During the post-rut, I often hunt in a different transition zone than where I hunted during the rut. I hang my stand as close to a bedding area as possible at least a month before the post-rut.

Post-Rut Calling: Although rattling and grunting work best in November, don't put your calls away after the rut. Through the years, I've had many close encounters with bucks because I rattled and called during the post-rut.

When rattling during the post-rut, imitate a sparring match instead of a full-blown fight. Bucks seldom participate in full-blown fights after the rut, so less noise generally works better. Tickling the tines or lightly banging the antlers together will do the job.

Bucks are wary by December, so your setup is critical. Because you'll be close to the bedding

Left: Button bucks should be protected in any QDM program. Before you shoot an antlerless deer, make sure it isn't a young buck.

area, you don't need to rattle loudly. Also, set up in thick cover and have a clear shooting lane downwind from your stand because bucks often circle downwind as they try to locate combatants.

Although I love to rattle in the post-rut, I prefer grunting and bleating just as I did during the pre-rut and rut.

SHOULD YOU HUNT FOOD PLOTS?

One of the by-products of my research with Laroche is the opportunity to observe hourly deer movements throughout autumn. In our study, data collected by 12 trail-timer monitors revealed that more than 55 percent of deer activity on aggressively managed QDM land occurred during the day. On the other hand, the timers set up in high-pressure areas told a different story. In those areas, more than 70 percent of deer movement occurred at night. This contrast illustrates the benefits of low-impact hunting.

Pre-Rut: Unlike during the rut, when bucks are ballistic and constantly on the move, deer activity during the pre-rut can be slow and inconsistent. Evening tends to be more productive than morning because warm temperatures keep deer bedded all day. As the coolness of night approaches, they become eager to feed.

Rut: When the rut is at its peak, expect action throughout the day. However, dawn to noon and the last two hours of the day are the magic times for buck action.

Post-rut: A whitetail's feeding times in the post-rut can change drastically from what they were in September, October and November. In the North, where winter usually begins in early December, deer will be more active during midday, especially on aggressively managed QDM lands where hunting pressure is not intense. I've found that 10 a.m. to 2 p.m. and 3 p.m. to dusk offer the greatest deer movement.

Weather's Role: Whitetails and other wildlife can detect impending weather changes. Deer can tell when the barometer is falling even if the sky is clear. Because of this, they feed more before bad weather.

Whitetails typically move more when the barometer is moving than when it is steady, and the greatest movement occurs when the barometer drops rapidly. With few exceptions, deer move little after a front arrives. Then, as the front passes and the weather stabilizes, whitetails and other wildlife begin moving in search of food.

Several research projects have studied the effects of barometric pressure on whitetail activity. Illinois biologist Keith Thomas found that whitetails fed the most when the barometer was

Far left: You must control the antlerless deer population, otherwise the habitat and buck population will suffer. **Left:** Some QDM programs let young hunters kill any legal deer on their first hunt.

between 29.8 and 30.29 inches.

Warm temperatures shut down rutting activity in a heartbeat. Of all rut suppressors, temperature might have the most influence on daytime deer activity.

Laroche and I use a sophisticated temperature monitor in our research. Every four minutes from October through December, the device records air temperature in the research area. With the aid of trail timers, we've seen that deer movement slows considerably when the temperature is above 45 degrees. When it hovers between 25 and 35 degrees, activity is high, especially during the rut.

FOOD SOURCES

The decision to hunt food sources boils down to how much you want to educate deer and whether you want to risk spooking deer onto neighboring properties. Of course, on larger properties, this isn't a problem, but for most landowners it's a serious consideration.

If you hunt food sources, you will put deer on high alert, and they might go nocturnal. Man is the whitetail's worst enemy, and if deer continually encounter humans in an area, they will stay out of it during the day.

However, hunting food sources can be productive if you figure out how to get to and from your stand. Food plots can be great in late afternoon, assuming you arrive well before deer show up.

Exiting a food plot can be challenging, so consider these basic approaches: Wait until deer leave

---

Left: In fine-tuned QDM programs, rub lines are often found in funnels and travel corridors, which are good places to ambush a rutting buck.

the food plot, wait until nightfall or have someone pick you up with an all-terrain vehicle. The ATV will spook deer off the plot, and let you exit unnoticed. Because most deer are somewhat accustomed to vehicles, an ATV is less threatening than a hunter. So, deer often return to the food plot within a half-hour of the ATV's departure.

Also, rake leaves and debris off the trail to your stand for a silent entrance and exit.

Deercoying: On QDM land, decoys can be very effective on food plots. If you use a doe decoy, place it 20 to 25 yards in front of your stand so you are looking at the decoy's rump.

A buck decoy should be about 30 yards away, facing you. Also, make sure the buck's antlers are similar to antler sizes in your area.

In either case, secure the decoy to the ground and spray it with a scent eliminator. And, never leave it in the field when you are not present.

To make the decoy more effective, add motion. Try attaching a white handkerchief to the decoy's rump. Run monofilament from the handkerchief to your stand, and periodically give the line a slight tug. The handkerchief will look like a wagging tail, which adds realism.

WHEN TO STAY OUT

Recovering wounded deer is generally a daytime task. However, on QDM land, that's usually not the case. If a wounded deer runs into a sanctuary, don't try to locate it during the day. If your property is less than 300 acres, you could disrupt the deer population at the least desirable time and force deer to flee the property. All too often, daytime tracking on small QDM parcels lets neighboring landowners shoot "protected" bucks that flee from trackers.

The best way to ensure that neighboring landowners don't kill "your" deer is to avoid pressuring deer during the day. Wounded deer should only be recovered under the cover of darkness. This might not be the most convenient way to track deer, but it will ensure you don't compromise your goals. Good tracking lights are necessary when you have to look for a deer at night.

END NOTE

My book, *Hunting Whitetails by the Moon*, details the research Laroche and I conducted on the moon's effects on whitetail movement and behavior. The book also details how I hunt whitetails, including the successful strategies I've used for more than 40 years. Autographed copies of this book and my other books can be purchased at www.charlesalsheimer.com. ■

Right: QDM lets hunters enjoy deer hunting in ways they never imagined.

CHAPTER 17

Commercial QDM

U p to this point, I've only addressed managing and hunting your own property. However, I've met many people who want the benefits of QDM without owning or working a piece of land. For them, the only options are being invited to hunt QDM property or booking a hunt with an outfitter who practices QDM. Unfortunately, such outfitters aren't easy to find.

Since 1990, I've questioned prospective outfitters about their QDM philosophies, which helps me sort out outfitters with better hunting opportunities. I've even hunted with some only to realize they didn't practice what they preached. From experience, I know many operations that claim to embrace QDM fall short of what I think QDM should be.

One of the biggest faults with QDM outfitters is that they book too many hunters for the amount of land they control. This almost always results in hunters killing too many immature bucks. These outfitters also fail to control the doe population.

Legitimate commercial QDM operations are few and far between. However, I believe this will change as outfitters realize how QDM can enhance their businesses. I've included a description of the two best QDM outfitters I've hunted with in the past 10 years. Both understand what it takes to produce quality bucks, and both work diligently to ensure their clients experience all the benefits of QDM.

QDM SOUTHERN STYLE

QDM originated in Texas. On ranches managed for QDM, large-racked whitetails are abundant, which makes the Texas brush country one of the best places to hunt commercial QDM deer.

Texas probably won't be like what you expect. When I first looked into hunting South Texas, I envisioned a forsaken place with impenetrable brush and desert-like conditions. South Texas certainly has the brush and it can be dry, but, oh, what natural beauty! And, I've been to few places in North America where wildlife is more abundant.

I've seen some well-managed operations, but the Retamosa Ranch run by the Hefner Appling family is as good as it gets. Many years ago, my friend Erwin Bauer hunted the Retamosa and wrote about it in *Outdoor Life*. In his article, Bauer shared how he killed a big white-tailed buck at the ranch. He nicknamed the ranch "Senderos," meaning the deer were as big as Texas. He wasn't wrong.

When I first saw the Retamosa in 1989, I thought I was in whitetail heaven. Located just north of Laredo, the Retamosa's 5,000 acres include some of the thickest brush country I've seen. The ranch includes extensive food plots that provide deer with a year-round buffet of nutritious food.

Right: It's possible to shoot bucks like this on good commercial QDM land. The author killed this whitetail in December 2000 while hunting with Saskatchewan outfitter Bentley Brown.

From a deer-management standpoint, the Applings monitor their deer population extensively and aggressively harvest does to ensure the adult-doe-to-antlered-buck ratio is close to 1-to-1. The ranch accommodations are outstanding, and the only thing better is the quality of the deer.

I've included three days from my 1994 diary, which should give an idea of what the Retamosa is like. During this time, I hunted on a trophy-management hunt, meaning I could only kill an 8- or 9-pointer. Anything bigger was off-limits.

Day 1, Dec. 16 — With overcast skies and a temperature of 70 degrees, Hefner Appling Sr. and I set up my decoy in the pre-dawn darkness before climbing into our stand overlooking a series of senderos, or long, narrow openings. As night faded to dawn, deer began showing in three senderos. At first light, a 160-class 11-pointer chased a doe through the brush 100 yards away. This buck was off-limits for me. In the next two hours, I saw 15 does and fawns and seven more bucks between 125- and 135-inches — nothing I wanted to shoot.

Below: The author killed this buck at the Retamosa Ranch in Texas.

With the temperature rising, we headed back to the lodge for lunch. In the afternoon, I went to a different stand with Sprague Sommers, one of Hefner's guides. I set up the decoy and waited. Despite the overcast skies, the temperature was rising, so I didn't expect much movement. I was right. Only a yearling 5-pointer and a doe and fawn showed up. Day 1 recap: 21 does and fawns; 11 bucks.

Day 2, Dec. 17 — The temperature dropped to 54 degrees last night. With overcast and cool conditions, I was sure deer would move. Not so. I saw six bucks and nine does and fawns, but no shooters. The afternoon was different. A cool breeze came up and the temperature lingered around 60 degrees. I saw 16 does and fawns and six bucks, including a mature 12-pointer I couldn't shoot. The rut was obviously kicking in. When I got back to camp I learned that Brian Crawford from Albany, N.Y., had killed a perfect 10-pointer that grossed around 160 B&C. Day 2 recap: 25 does and fawns; 12 bucks.

Day 3, Dec. 18 — The weather was the same as Day 2 — 54 degrees and overcast at dawn. I hunted until 11 a.m. because bucks were on the prowl. While I sat, I saw many does, fawns and bucks. For the first two hours, a 160-class 12-pointer chased does in and out of the senderos. What a sight, even though he was off-limits.

At about 8:30 a.m., I witnessed a first. About 450 yards down a fence line from my stand, a big deer jumped the cattle fence. By the time I brought up my binoculars, a 160-class 10-pointer went under the fence. Fifteen yards behind him was the biggest buck I've seen in the wild. I've scored enough racks to know that bruiser had at least 200 inches of bone on his head. His G-2s were 14- to 15-inches with mule deer forks. Though the rack was only 16 to 17 inches wide, it had trash everywhere. An incredible whitetail! An incredible morning!

When we returned to the lodge for lunch, the camp was admiring a perfect 160-class 12-pointer killed earlier by Mitch Rhodes of Jacksonville, Fla.

My afternoon hunt was better than the morning. With no wind and cool conditions, I moved to a stand where another hunter had seen plenty of activity in the morning. With an hour of light left, a mature buck crossed the sendero about 250 yards away. I picked up my antlers and rattled loud and hard, trying to bring him toward my decoy.

Within a minute of finishing, I noticed movement to my right — it was the buck that had crossed the sendero. His hair stood on end as he strutted through the brush. He was going to step into the sendero near the decoy.

When the big 9-pointer entered the sendero, he was a few feet from the decoy. Surprisingly, the buck hadn't seen the decoy until he stepped into the opening, and it scared him to death. He panicked as he tried to escape, and he never offered me a shot.

Below: Saskatchewan is the place to go if you want to hunt big bucks. Plus, you'll find several commercial QDM operations there.

When I got back to camp, Steve Moak from Missouri was driving in with a huge typical 9-pointer he had killed just before nightfall. The buck was a dandy, grossing 156 B&C. Day 3 recap: 22 does and fawns; 11 bucks.

The remaining two days were like the first three. In 1989, I had killed a great 9-pointer on the second day of my hunt at the ranch. However, this hunt was different. Although I didn't kill a buck, my trip to the Retamosa was incredible. In five days, I passed up several 130-class bucks. The way I look at it, I didn't lose; I just ran out of time. I saw some incredible bucks and learned how the

Applings manage their ranch and practice QDM. It's truly a place to hunt for the buck of a lifetime.

If you're interested in hunting the South Texas brush country, remember that the rut is in December. Contact Appling Farms, Box 1387, El Campo, TX 77437, or call (979) 543-4301.

QDM NORTHERN STYLE

Outfitter Bentley Brown of Saskatchewan runs the Northern location I think best exemplifies commercial QDM. Although Brown cannot plant food plots or aggressively manage does in his 80,000-acre area, the results he gets are as good as most QDM operations.

Brown is located on the fringe of farm country. Nonresident hunters cannot hunt the farm zone, but Brown's area is close enough to it that the whitetails benefit from the agriculture. Because Brown's hunting area is so large, the 30 to 35 bucks his clients kill each year have little effect on the deer population. Instead, wolves, coyotes and severe winters keep deer in balance with the range's carrying capacity.

Based on hunter/outfitter surveys, the area has about 15 to 20 deer per square mile with an adult-doe-to-antlered-buck ratio close to 1-to-1. So,

15 Questions For Booking a QDM Hunt

- What is the outfitter's opinion of QDM? What does he know?

- How big is the hunting area?

- How many hunters does he take per week and for the season?

- How long is the hunt?

- How big are the bucks clients kill? What are the ages and weights?

- Will you be expected to shoot does?

- How many stands does he use, and how far apart are they?

- What kind of equipment does the outfitter use — trucks, quads, stands?

- Does he plant food plots or use supplemental feeding?

- What hunting strategy does he use — stands, drives, still-hunting?

- Ask him to walk you through a day of hunting.

- What are the accommodations and food like?

- Will he pick you up at the airport or are you responsible for your own transportation?

- How much does the hunt cost? What tips are expected?

- Get a list of references from successful and unsuccessful hunters.

everything about Brown's setup — from the habitat to the deer herd to the bucks his hunters harvest — lines up with the definition of QDM. I've hunted with Brown five times, and on each occasion, the experience was special and the bucks I killed were heart-stoppers.

Brown's food, accommodations, equipment and guides are excellent. However, there are some shortcomings. November in Saskatchewan can be an endurance test for hunters. I've hunted the province several times, and I know it's no place for a hunter who hates snow and cold. However, if you want to hunt some of the biggest whitetails on the planet, this is the place to go.

So, what's Saskatchewan like? I'll use excerpts from my 2000 diary to give you an idea.

Day 3 of a six-day hunt, Nov. 29 — It was overcast and 8 degrees with a slight breeze out of the east when Bentley dropped me off at a stand called Kevin's. Three inches of snow covered the ground. As is my custom when hunting Canada, I burrowed deep into my oversized sleeping bag to stay warm. Because of the clouds, daybreak was a long time coming. When I could finally make out my surroundings, I liked what I saw. The stand was in what Bentley described as a prime travel corridor, and aside from the dense brush and aspen to the left of the stand, the woods was choked with thick spruce.

Except for an occasional magpie and raven overhead, I didn't see anything the first two

Left: The author killed this buck while hunting with Bentley Brown. It's the author's biggest buck to date, scoring 175 B&C.

hours. At 10:15 a.m., three does and two fawns passed through followed by a yearling 8-pointer about a half-hour later. For the next six hours, small bucks, does and fawns passed back and forth within 75 yards of my stand. At 5:20 p.m., a 140-class 9-pointer poked through the timber. If it had been the last day of the hunt, I'd have taken him. However, I passed. Day 3 recap: 14 does and fawns; 10 bucks.

Day 4, Nov. 30 — I liked the stand so much that I asked Bentley to let me hunt it again. Conditions were similar to the previous day — overcast, slight breeze out of the east, 18 degrees. Throughout the day, it seemed to warm up although I didn't know the temperature. Deer activity was about the same as the previous day. At 4:30 p.m., a heavy-bodied 125- to 130-inch 10-pointer slowly walked by at 50 yards. It was obvious he had been fighting because his ear and neck were smeared with blood. I let him go.

On the way to camp, Bentley told me his plans.

"I'm going to have you try a different stand tomorrow," he said. "Some nasty weather is supposed to roll in, and I think you might have better luck at a stand we call Sunshine North."

Day 4 recap: 10 does and fawns; 8 bucks.

Day 5, Dec. 1 — Bentley hit the nail on the head! The weather took a turn for the worse during the night. At breakfast, I noticed the thermometer outside the kitchen window read 5 degrees. With wind gusting from 10 to 20 mph, I knew my work was cut out for me.

In the dark, the two-mile quad ride from the trailhead to the stand was anything but pleasant as wind and snow pecked at my face. At my stand, I tried to get comfortable as I shifted around inside the sleeping bag. When dawn finally arrived, I knew the day would be a real gut check. Because of the snow, wind and temperature, I doubted I'd see any deer. My big challenge was

trying to figure out how I could stay on stand all day in such conditions.

Three hours had passed since my guide, Chris Lavoie, positioned me in Sunshine North. As the big spruce holding the stand swayed in the wind, I wondered if I'd be able to stay put for seven hours. The temperature was near zero, and my hands and face were stinging from wind gusts approaching 20 mph. I remember thinking the conditions were better for polar bears than whitetails.

At about 10:30 a.m., heavy snow began falling, so I hunkered into the oversized sleeping bag. I couldn't imagine deer would be moving, but I was wrong.

Before that thought drifted away, my luck changed. To my left, about 70 yards away in open

Above: When planning a hunt, make sure the outfitter has good guides, the right equipment, good herd age structure and knows whitetails as well as you do. Brown's operation – shown here – and the Retamosa Ranch fulfill all four categories.

hardwoods, I saw a deer walking through a stand of mature aspen and spruce. Despite the distance, I spotted antlers against the snowy backdrop. Time was of the essence, so fumbling for binoculars to count points was out of the question. I knew he was big. In one motion, I slid my frozen .270 into position, clicked off the safety, put the cross-hairs behind the buck's front shoulder and squeezed. At the roar of the rifle, the big buck jumped and then exploded into the thick brush.

In seconds, I went from freezing to nearly sweating. After gaining my composure, I descended from the stand and followed the buck's trail. Within 30 yards, I came upon one of the biggest bucks I'd seen in the wild. He was a Saskatchewan bruiser in every way. His antlers grossed a shade

more than 170 B&C. He was the only deer I saw that day, but overall, I saw 25 bucks. During the week, all eight hunters in camp killed bucks scoring 147 to 189 B&C. Like the other four hunts I'd taken with Brown, he and his guides had gone the extra mile to make sure I went home with wonderful memories. If you're looking for a Northern hunt with QDM flavor, this is it.

Contact Brown at Box 475, Turtleford, Saskatchewan, Canada, S0M 2Y0, or call (306) 845-2444. ▪

CHAPTER 18

The Social Side of QDM: Selling the Vision

Salesmanship is a powerful thing, especially in QDM. In my writings and lectures, I often share the saying, "Nothing happens until something is sold."

Those who practice QDM quickly realize that managing deer is much easier than managing people. Deer can be controlled, but people are another story because they have minds of their own and often resist change.

I'll never forget how Al Brothers wined and dined me with his QDM sales pitch in December 1989. For an entire day, as we bounced around the Jambers Ranch in his pickup, he pumped me full of the words, phrases and concepts that describe QDM. Then, at the end of the day, he sealed the deal by saying, "Charlie, I'll tell you what I'm going to do. I'm going to buy you a membership in the Quality Deer Management Association of America."

Brothers hooked me with his words and commitment to QDM. His wildlife management background is legendary, but I think he's as good a salesman as he is a biologist.

How you sell QDM is crucial to its success. Quite simply, if you can't handle the people factor, the program won't succeed.

THE PUBLIC

Approaching the public with QDM can be touchy. I'll never forget the first two seminars held by our fledgling Steuben County group. The first went smoothly, and no one in the audience voiced disapproval with what we were proposing.

A couple of weeks later, we were asked to speak to a group in a bordering county. During the question-and-answer segment, several people voiced disapproval of any type of QDM. One person accused us of trying to turn New York into "an Illinois," where the common man can't hunt because land is leased to the wealthy.

Another called QDM the worst type of deer management ever devised. Two other attendees also chimed in with negative comments. I'm sure those four individuals left many people in the audience scratching their heads.

For QDM organizers, it's frustrating how slowly the public accepts the concepts of QDM. From experience, I know it feels like you take two steps forward and one step backward. There will always be dissenters, but a little planning can keep them minimal.

Be Organized: The best salespeople have a vision and a plan. Having a plan is critical when selling QDM to hunters. The benefits of QDM must take center stage, and the concept always works where it is given a chance. It's hard for the public to refute better habitat, more mature bucks, a more balanced sex ratio and better hunters in the field.

Think Long Term: Realize that selling QDM will take time. Rome wasn't built in a day, and getting the public to embrace QDM might take

years. It's important not to hurry the process.

Keep the Fire Lit: When the fire goes out, it's not easy to rekindle. Keep QDM and its virtues before the public. In Steuben County, we do this by holding an annual Antler Round Up and sending out a quarterly newsletter. The newsletter keeps members aware of the chapter's progress and offers tips on how to improve. By drawing attention to QDM and its successes, we keep the fire lit.

Set a Good Example: The phrase "more is caught than taught" often applies to raising children, but it is also true in QDM. Setting a good example for fellow hunters can be far more convincing than lecturing them on whitetail management. Now that our QDM group is nearing its 10th anniversary, we have a proven track record. The fruits of our labor have converted those who were skeptical when we first shared our ideas.

The annual Antler Round Up provides proof. First, we educate attendees about the benefits of QDM, and then we show them bucks from the previous year killed under the county's QDM program. This gets their attention, just like John Mills' buck captured the attention of a handful of landowners 10 years ago.

Don't Be Pushy: One of the worst things you can do during a QDM sales pitch is to push the concept on people. It won't work! Save your energy, because people — especially hunters and country folk — don't like to be told what to do or that what they're doing is wrong.

Being pushy irritates people. As Kenny Rogers sang, "You have to know when to hold 'em and know when to fold 'em." It's important to know when and how to play your QDM cards. By breaking down the concept and presenting it in bite-size pieces, you'll be more successful. Also, even though it's wise to slowly introduce someone to QDM, make sure you're consistently promoting the concept. QDM is a yearlong endeavor

Left: The author presents the QDM message at one of his deer-hunting seminars. A big portion of the seminar deals with QDM and its benefits. Below: More hunters are discovering the benefits of QDM.

— it cannot shut down when deer season ends.

Convincing landowners to start a QDM program is just the beginning. After this, a new set of issues crop up.

NEIGHBORS

QDM can create conflicts between neighbors. In addition to design and implementation, effectively dealing with these conflicts is important for a successful QDM program. If bickering occurs, a program can be severely affected.

Conflicts between neighboring landowners can range from simple to complex. Most problems are minor at first, but they can easily escalate into major confrontations. It doesn't take much for something small to turn into a border war.

It can be frustrating when a neighboring landowner places bait near property lines to attract your deer. Of course, food plots planted near property lines have the same effect. Controversy also arises when a non-QDM landowner (or marginal QDM player) places stands along a property line in hopes of killing bucks passed up by a QDM neighbor. In my experience, this is the No. 1 problem mentioned by frustrated QDM participants.

Comments usually sound like this: "It's so frustrating to see how our neighbors take advantage of what we're trying to do. They know full well that we pass on 1^1/$_2$- and 2^1/$_2$-year-old bucks. So, what do they do? They hang stands along our boundary line so they can get a crack at the bucks we're trying to save."

If you own property, it's easy to think the deer on your land are yours. This is why it can be so frustrating when you "feed 'em and sleep 'em" but your neighbors hunt 'em. In reality, unless your neighbor is breaking the law, you can't stop him. Instead, figure out what motivates the person and use it to your advantage. This can be slow, but it works.

One of our neighbors thought it was OK to hang stands near our property line and shoot at any legal deer that crossed the line. He knew I was trying to improve the age structure of the bucks,

but he continued to think that any deer that set foot on his property deserved a dose of lead.

Then, things began to change. He saw some of the bucks we were killing. I even took him around and showed him the food plots I'd planted, and I followed this up by inviting him to our Steuben County Antler Round Up. It wasn't long before he became interested in practicing QDM on his property.

He cleared some land and planted food plots. Now, after several years of watching, he's raising the bar on his QDM vision. It would have been easy to raise a stink. Instead, I tried a different

approach by showing him a better way to manage and enjoy whitetails.

When neighboring landowners work together (even if their harvest guidelines are different), great things can happen. My home county is a classic example. Another great example is Buffalo County in western Wisconsin, a nationally recognized illustration of the potential of QDM. Until a few years ago, Buffalo County deer hunters subscribed to the classic "if it's brown, it's down" mentality. Today, thousands of acres of land are being managed for better sex ratios, age structure and food sources. And,

Above: The Annual Antler Round Up in Steuben County, N.Y., is a great crowd attractor – and a great way for organizers to promote QDM.

some incredible bucks are killed there.

Why the rapid change? Just like our Steuben County movement, when people in Buffalo County saw the results of their neighbors' efforts, they latched onto the vision of QDM.

The tough part is selling the QDM concept, but once that happens, the rewards can be substantial. Seize every opportunity to share the benefits of QDM. A little nudging might be all you need to convince your neighbors that their hunting will improve through QDM.

MEMBERS WITHIN THE GROUP

You'd think QDM would be easy to sell to members of your group or people who hunt your property. Unfortunately, this isn't always the case. Anyone who has instituted a QDM program has had a member or guest who didn't follow property rules. Sadly, those in charge of the program often overreact, and tensions flare when the wrong buck is killed.

Restrain your emotions if this happens. When calm, gather your thoughts and turn the situation into a teaching experience by sharing why the buck shouldn't have been killed. This will reduce the chance of small bucks being killed in the future and will let you maintain positive relationships with fellow hunters.

If the same hunter continues to break the rules, it's obvious he doesn't have the program's best interest at heart or, worse yet, doesn't care. For the good of

the program, he should be asked to leave the group. If the violator is a guest, do not invite him back.

STATE AGENCIES

In the early '90s, QDM was so new to the Northeast that many individuals within New York's Department of Environmental Conservation were a bit skeptical. Only two of the original 12 members of our group had any formal training in wildlife biology and management. From the negative comments we received,

it was obvious we were viewed as radical landowners with little knowledge of how to manage whitetails.

In retrospect, it's easy to see why some state officials saw us this way. Amateur biologists often offend trained biologists. For the most part, those questioning us had spent their careers studying whitetails and felt that traditional management was better than what the "new kids on the block" had proposed.

Managing whitetails is not rocket science, and I've seen many examples of deer herds from Texas to New York that have been improved without the help of wildlife professionals. However, I don't mean that a management program should be attempted without the aid of a professional.

When dealing with government wildlife agencies, don't offend them. Their ranks are made up of good, talented people, many of whom are interested in seeing QDM succeed. Just remember, wildlife agencies seldom change overnight.

Also, organize a group of like-minded landowners and present your plan to state agencies in a positive manner. Be sure to approach state wildlife experts in a non-threatening way, otherwise you won't be received positively. It's easier to encourage change when you are organized and have numbers on your side. Like politicians, state wildlife agencies often march to the beat of the crowd — just remember to keep the crowd cordial and orderly.

From Georgia to Michigan and Arkansas, organized QDM groups have brought significant changes to whitetail management. In nearly every successful case, the road was winding and full of potholes, but they overcame the obstacles to bring about a better way to manage America's favorite deer.

Selling QDM is never easy, but if done with sensitivity and purpose, it is possible. There is no perfect way to promote QDM to the public, but good people skills almost always lead to better results.

Left: One of the greatest challenges to hunting, is finding a place to hunt. Every year, more land is placed off-limits to hunters.

CHAPTER 19

The Future of QDM

For years, I dreamed of the day quality bucks would walk the fields of western New York. Unfortunately, Northeastern hunters tend to subscribe to a philosophy that can be summed up in one phrase: "If it's brown, it's down." It is not uncommon for 80 percent to 90 percent of the antlered deer harvest in the Northeast to be $1^1/_2$-year-old bucks.

Gradually, though, this mentality has changed. Mature bucks are more common now that hunters realize there is a better way to manage whitetails. One of the biggest factors contributing to this is the evolution of the deer hunter.

The average deer hunter is 45 years old, and this figure is rising. Research from Cornell University shows that sportsman go through five stages. In the first two, hunters shoot any deer and, ultimately, want to limit out. In the third stage, their priority is killing a trophy animal. During the final stages, sportsmen mellow out and become engrossed in hunting methods. Most deer hunters are firmly entrenched in the last two phases, which is why QDM is attractive. QDM has also been helped by the fact that today's sportsmen are better educated and have more resources than previous generations.

Some hunters still travel to faraway places to hunt big bucks, but more and more are opting to stay home and get involved in all aspects of whitetail hunting. Developing and managing your own land for quality deer can be tremen-

dously satisfying, and because of this, QDM's future looks bright.

When preparing to write this book, I asked Craig Dougherty of North Country Whitetails about this. Dougherty has spent a lifetime in the deer woods as a hunter, landowner and land manager.

"I'm convinced that the future of deer hunting will be tightly tied to QDM," he said, "because I don't think hunters will be content settling for just any deer. Our deer populations are at a point where hunters can be more selective, and today's deer hunters want the challenge of hunting mature bucks.

"As hunters age, they want to bring other dimensions into their hunt, and nothing in my lifetime has rivaled the role of QDM. As we look to the future, I believe there will be a shift in our essential values. We will place a greater emphasis on stewardship, and QDM is a natural for this.

"The basic tenet of shooting does — and lots of them — is a real plus for those who like venison, as well as for those who are new to the sport. The fact that young hunters have more opportunities to kill deer speaks volumes for QDM. QDM has something for everyone, and that's a big reason why I'm so excited about it."

I asked Dougherty about the obstacles that stand in the way of QDM.

"One of the biggest challenges for QDM is to get state recognition so that public lands can reap

the rewards of QDM," he said. "This will take creative thinking by state officials. Otherwise, the concept will forever be tied to the wallet."

Dougherty concluded by pointing out that QDM is about more than deer.

"There is something inside everyone that drives them to reach out and touch the world they live in," he said, "so impacting the land and growing things is important. Man is most satisfied when he acts as a steward, and QDM is a good way to be a steward."

Thousands of deer hunters across America share these feelings, and more hunters embrace QDM every year. Through the tireless efforts of the Quality Deer Management Association, the QDM message is spreading to every state inhabited by whitetails. The organization's seminars, displays and quarterly magazine, *Quality*

Right: Today's hunters are looking for new dimensions in their hunts, and nothing can rival the benefits of QDM. **Below:** QDM promotes killing antlerless deer, which provides good opportunities for young hunters.

Whitetails, educate and inspire those who strive for better deer management.

Ten years ago, QDM could have been compared to a faint echo in the wilderness. It only received serious consideration in Texas and portions of the Southeast. In little more than a decade, the concept has exploded. Several state agencies have included QDM in their whitetail management plans, and many more are investigating some form of QDM. This has occurred because QDM is a common sense, biologically sound management method.

The direction of QDM was best summed up by Brian Murphy, executive director of the QDMA: "With the increasing challenges facing the future of deer hunting and management, such as increasing deer populations, declining hunter numbers and continued threats from animal-rights and gun-control groups, the QDMA is increasingly well-equipped to face these and other challenges. Clearly, QDM has arrived and will be the dominant management strategy as we progress through the 21st century."

Although QDM received mixed reviews a decade ago, the time is right for it to become the preeminent management philosophy. In some areas, QDM will continue to advance at a snail's pace. In other, more progressive areas, QDM will be embraced rapidly. Regardless, it is here to stay.

QDM works when it is given a chance. It is simply a better way to manage whitetails. ▪

Left: QDM emphasizes a balanced adult-doe-to-antlered-buck ratio, which is beneficial for hunters, state game departments and America's deer herds.

CHAPTER 20

QDM Q&A

As mentioned earlier, I was first exposed to quality deer management in 1989 when I met Al Brothers while hunting and photographing in Texas. I asked a lot of questions during my time with him, and the answers he provided convinced me that QDM was a better alternative to traditional deer management. Since then, as I've tried to spread the QDM message in my writings and seminars, I've fielded many questions from interested sportsmen. Following is a synopsis of the previous chapters, presented in question-and-answer format. By knowing the answers to these questions, you'll become a better advocate of QDM.

QDM BASICS

Q: What is quality deer management?
A: In a nutshell, QDM is a form of deer management that produces quality does, fawns and bucks. Yearling and 2-year-old bucks are protected to produce mature males, and doe harvesting is emphasized to control the adult-doe-to-antlered-buck ratio. In addition, the practice strives to keep deer habitat at a quality level. QDM also improves landowner relations and creates quality hunters. The end result is a quality hunt.

Q: Why is QDM becoming so popular?
A: QDM's popularity can be attributed to older, more-educated hunters. As hunters age, they seek ways to improve their hunting experience. One of the best methods is land and deer herd management.

Q: Is quality deer hunting different from trophy deer hunting?
A: Yes. In many cases, trophy hunting pays less attention to habitat and herd composition. QDM is more comprehensive because it addresses habitat creation and harvest management. Many trophy hunters want to kill big bucks without considering the land's carrying capacities or the adult-doe-to-antlered-buck ratio. QDM emphasizes mature bucks as well as habitat creation and balanced sex ratios.

CHEMISTRY FOR QUALITY BUCKS

Q: What is needed to produce quality bucks?
A: Age, genetics, good nutrition and herd management. Of these four, age and nutrition are the most important. After bucks reach maturity, they are what they eat in most instances, so the two go hand-in-hand.

Q: What is a "quality" buck?
A: A quality buck is mature or near maturity. Bucks generally need at least three years to get to this point. During the first three years, bucks use nutrients to build bones and muscles. Only after their bodies are fully developed do bucks produce their best antlers.

Q: Are spikes genetically inferior?
A: Not usually. The old adage "once a spike, always a spike" couldn't be further from the truth. A yearling buck grows spike antlers for seven primary reasons, and only one of those involves genetics. A

yearling spike buck is equivalent to a 12-year-old boy. Because his body is still in its early stages of development, it is difficult to predict what he could become. Not until age 3 or 4 do you get a good idea of his potential.

Q: What is an acceptable adult-doe-to-antlered-buck ratio?
A: Most biologists agree that a ratio of 1-to-1 or 2-to-1 is a good goal. However, most also agree that a 3-to-1 adult-doe-to-antlered-buck ratio can provide good QDM results. When the ratio goes beyond that, any semblance of a quality deer herd begins to disappear because the bucks become worn down and overall herd health suffers.

Q: Many hunters think it is wrong to kill does because more does result in more buck fawns. Is this correct?
A: This is a flawed assumption. Deer eat 1 to 2 tons of food per year, so the land can only support so many deer. When does are protected, bucks become overpressured and overharvested, which often forces yearlings to do most of the breeding. If too many does are in an area and the buck population is limited, not all does are bred when they come into estrus the first time, and they cycle again 28 days later. Consequently, the rut is drawn out and fawns are born a month or more later than normal. Also, because bucks are severely stressed, their antlers are usually stunted the following year. To prevent this, does must be killed to maintain a balanced herd.

WHERE DOES QDM WORK?

Q: Where does QDM work?
A: QDM works in nearly every corner of the whitetail's range, although some areas are better than others. In many parts of America, state game departments are reluctant to implement QDM. Therefore, private landowners must organize and work together to carry out the practice.

Left: It's critical that whitetails have balanced, year-round food sources. Food plots can provide this and more.

Q: Where won't QDM work?
A: QDM is difficult to implement without government help on large tracts of public land. Hunters who use public land tend to be more reluctant to pass up small bucks, because they think someone else will kill the buck. Also, because they are not landowners and don't have a vested interest in the deer herd, public-land hunters are less likely to care about the herd's quality.

ORGANIZING THE MOVEMENT

Q: How do you get a QDM program off the ground?
A: There are several ways. If you own more than 150 to 200 acres with good food, water and cover, you just have to convince yourself to start. However, there is power in numbers, and much more can be accomplished if other landowners join. So, the best way to start a QDM program is to meet with landowners, present the vision, establish guidelines and implement the plan.

Q: How much land do I need for QDM to work?
A: A rule of thumb is 1,000 contiguous acres. However, QDM will work with much less. Many successful QDM programs are on as little as 125 acres. Few people own 1,000 acres, so cooperation among neighboring landowners is essential.

Q: What if local landowners don't want to join?
A: QDM will still work. Actually, most QDM land is not contiguous, especially in the Northeast. Where I live, some land is under QDM and some is not, which creates a checkerboard appearance in an aerial photo when QDM properties are marked. The key to success for landowners that practice QDM in a "checkerboard landscape" is the ability to hold deer on properties they manage. You can achieve this by planting nutritional food sources on at least 2 percent to 5 percent of the property, setting aside at least one-third of the property as a sanctuary, and adopting low-pressure hunting techniques. Access to certain parts of the property, such as a sanctuary, should be limited during the season, and drive- and still-hunting should be abolished.

Q: *When should bucks be killed?*
A: Guidelines vary from one landowner to the next. Some QDM groups protect everything smaller than a 6-pointer. Others say that a buck must be at least an 8-pointer. On my property, a buck must be at least an 8-pointer with a 16-inch inside spread. For our area, this criteria means most bucks are at least 3 years old, which is the age class I prefer to hunt. Without the spread minimum, I risk killing an 8-point yearling. A yearling of this size almost always has superior genetics and needs to mature so he can reach his potential and pass on his genes.

Q: *Are there exceptions?*
A: Again, every group has its own rules. However, in most cases, young or first-time hunters have the option to kill any legal buck. It is important that new hunters experience success before they deal with rules. After killing a buck or two, they will be in a better position to understand QDM.

Q: *How important is record keeping?*
A: Very important. If you don't know what you are killing or can't estimate how many deer you have on your property, it is difficult to manage your herd. It is critical to age the jawbone of every deer you kill. In addition, record deer sightings and make special note of sex and ages. This will make you a better manager.

THEY ARE WHAT THEY EAT

Q: *After a QDM plan is in place, what should I do about habitat?*
A: Whitetails eat a lot of food, so it is important they have a balanced diet. The best supplemental foods vary by region, but it is tough to beat top-performing clovers and other deer-oriented forages when it comes to planting food plots. It's critical that the forages provide nutrition year-round. A supplemental mineral mix is also important, especially during the critical antler-growing season.

Q: *Where should food plots be located?*
A: Try to keep your food plots away from neighboring land, especially if the owner does not practice QDM. The plots should be long, narrow and provide deer with nearby cover so they feel safe coming to the plot during daylight. Also, try to position the plots so they run north to south.

Q: *Is anything required besides food plots?*
A: Because whitetails need food throughout the year, it is important to provide adequate browse during winter. On my land, for example, I selectively cut ash, oak, apple, aspen, maple, sumac, basswood and white cedar, which are whitetail favorites. It's best to contact an independent forester or your state's conservation department for assistance. You might also want to plant some mast- and fruit-producing trees.

Above: Bucks, does and fawns thrive under QDM.

CHALLENGES OF QDM

Q: What are the biggest obstacles for QDM hunters?
A: The biggest hurdle is probably the tendency to kill too many immature bucks and not enough does. For QDM to reach its full potential, does must be kept in check.

Q: Are there any other problems?
A: Public perception is a significant obstacle, and it comes in many forms. You will always be faced with non-QDM hunters who try to take advantage of those who practice QDM. This usually involves hunters setting up their stands on or close to the boundaries of QDM land. Such hunters disregard the program practiced on the neighboring property. Instead, they view the situation as a golden opportu-nity to shoot a buck at the QDM landowner's expense. All too often, such hunters kill yearling and 2-year-old bucks that the QDM landowner is trying to protect. The end result is hard feelings between neighbors, which often escalates into a border war.

Q: Will QDM be around in 20 years?
A: Absolutely. As we move further into the 21st century, QDM is arguably the hottest topic in the whitetail world. In the quest to make deer hunting better, hunters across America are embracing the concept. It is exciting, challenging and makes hunters better stewards of the land God has entrusted to them. ▪

References

BOOKS - QDM RELATED
Aging and Judging Trophy Whitetails, Dr. James C. Kroll.

Amazing Whitetails, Mike Biggs, T.P.W., Inc.

Deer, edited by Gerlach, Atwater, Schnell, Stackpole Books.

Food Plots & Supplemental Feeding, Ben H. Koerth and Dr. James C. Kroll.

Producing and Harvesting White-tailed Deer, Kroll.

Producing Quality Whitetails, Al Brothers and Murphy E. Ray, Jr., Texas Wildlife Association.

Quality Whitetails, Karl V. Miller and R. Larry Marchinton, editors.

The Whitetail Chronicles, Mike Biggs, T.P.W., Inc.

White-tailed Deer – Ecology and Management, Lowell K. Halls, editor, Stackpole Books.

Whitetail: Behavior through the Seasons, Charles J. Alsheimer, Krause Publications.

Whitetail Spring, John Ozoga, Willow Creek Press.

Whitetail Summer, John Ozoga, Willow Creek Press.

Whitetail Autumn, John Ozoga, Willow Creek Press.

Whitetail Winter, John Ozoga, Willow Creek Press

Whitetail Intrigue, John Ozoga, Krause Publications.

Whitetails in Action, Mike Biggs, T.P.W., Inc.

BOOKS - HUNTING RELATED
Advanced Strategies for Trophy Whitetails, David Morris, Safari Press.

Hunting Trophy Deer, John Wootters, Revised edition Lyons and Burford, New York.

Hunting Whitetails by the Moon, Alsheimer, Krause Publications.

PUBLICATIONS
Quality Whitetails, official publication of the Quality Deer Management Association of America.

Whitetail News, official publication of the Whitetail Institute of North America.

Deer & Deer Hunting magazine, Krause Publications, 700 E. State St., Iola, WI 54990

ORGANIZATIONS
Quality Deer Management Association, Box 227, Watkinsville, GA 30677, (800) 209-3337, www.qdma.com

Farmers and Hunters Feeding the Hungry, 216 North Cleveland Ave., Hagerstown, MD 21740, (301)739-3000. www.fhfh.org.

Whitetail Institute of North America, Route 1, Box 3006, Pintala, AL 36043, (334) 281-3006, www.deer-nutrition.com

Whitetails Unlimited Inc., Box 720, Sturgeon Bay, WI 54235, (800) 274-5471, www.whitetailsunlimited.com

FEEDERS
American Hunter, 1013 Dalworth, Mesquite, TX 75149, (972) 285-7650, www.americanhunterfeeders.com

Moultrie Feeders, 150 Industrial Road, Alabaster, AL 35007, (800) 653-3334, www.moultriefeeders.com

Sweeney Feeders, 321 Waring-Welfare Road, Boerne, TX 78006-7927, (800) 443-4244, www.sweeney feeders.com

SEEDS AND MINERALS
Antler King Products, W11353 Spaulding Road, Black River Falls, WI 54615, (715) 284-9547, www.antlerking.com

IMPERIAL WHITETAIL CLOVER
The Whitetail Institute, Route 1, Box 3006, Pintala, AL 35043, (334) 281-3006, www.deernutrition.com

Mossy Oak BioLogic, Box 757, 200 E. Main St. West Point, MS 39773, (662) 494-8859, www.mossyoak.com

Pennington Seed, 1280 Atlanta Hwy., Box 290, Madison, GA 30650, (800) 285-SEED, www.penningtonseed.com

UAP Northeast, Box 93, Shults Ave., Cohocton, NY 14826, (716) 384-5221, www.uap.com

Wildlife Nutrition Systems, Box 449, Kenedy, TX 78119, (888) 355-9678, www.wnst.com

SEED/GROWTH ENHANCERS
Trophy Excellerator, 3898 West, Box 189, Jay, FL 32565, (800) 289-4953, www.scottsoutdoors.com

ATV IMPLEMENTS
The Plotmaster, Wood-N-Water, 311 N. Marcus, Wrightsville, GA 31096, (888) 440-9108, www.theplotmaster.com

Monroe Tufline, Box 186, Columbus, MS 39703, (662) 328-8347, www.monroetufline.com

TOOTH AGING LABORATORY
Buck-Tooth Labs, Box 13333, Edwardsville, KS 66113, (913) 441-8497

Matson's Laboratory, LLC, Box 308, Milltown, MT 59851, (406) 258-6286

PERSONALIZED TOPO MAPS
My Topo.Com, Expedition Maps, Box 2075, Red Lodge, MT 59068, (877) 587-9004, www.mytopo.com

OBSERVATION CAMERAS
Trail Timer Co., Box 28722, 5710 Memorial Ave. #3330, St. Paul, MN 55128, (651) 738-0925, www.trailtimer.com

CamTrak South, Inc., CamTrakker Cameras, 1050 Industrial Drive, Watkinsville, GA 30677, (800) 654-8498, www.camtrakker.com

DeerCam, QDMA, Box 227, Watkinsville, GA 30677, (800) 209-3337, www.qdma.com

QDM CONSULTANTS
Alsheimer Whitetails, 4730 Route 70A, Bath, NY 14810, (607) 566-2781, www.charlesalsheimer.com

North Country Whitetails, Box 925, Fairport, NY 14450, (716) 388-6990, www.northcountrywhitetails.com

RECORD-KEEPING MATERIALS
Quality Deer Management Association, Box 227, Watkinsville, GA 30677, (800) 209-3337, www.qdma.com

Boone and Crockett Club, 250 Station Drive, Missoula, MT 59801, (406) 542-1888, www.boone-crockett.org

Index

Acknowledgments

In September 1979, my life changed drastically. Within a few days, I went from a successful corporate sales and marketing career to communicating the outdoor experience with pen and camera. At the time, some of my friends and associates thought I had made a major mistake. Their rationale was: "Why leave such a good job for an 'iffy' career where few succeed?" I'll admit that early on, there were times when that weighed heavy on my mind.

Though my career change might have appeared irrational, my jump from the corporate to outdoor world has enriched my life beyond measure. The move has given me the blessing of having a dream career. Much of the success I've enjoyed has been because of the people I've met and worked with while pursuing all aspects of white-tailed deer.

I've heard it said that a man who fails to remember his past has no future. In assessing the path I've taken, I'm grateful and indebted to those who have made my career possible. At the risk of leaving someone out, I'd like to salute those who have helped make my QDM journey possible.

Carla: You're the love of my life and a wonderful wife. You've gone out of your way to encourage my QDM journey. Thanks for helping me chase my dream.

Aaron: You're the greatest son any man could hope to have. The role you've played in our QDM program has been special. Thanks for all the farm work, your doe hunting savvy and for the edit work you did on this book. I owe many of our QDM successes to you.

Charles H. Alsheimer: Thanks, Dad, for introducing me to hunting. Starting at age 5 you let me tag along with you on deer hunts. Though you're gone now, the memories we shared in the deer woods will remain with me forever.

Haas Hargrave: You're the greatest boss I've had. Your business savvy is unparalleled. The guidance you gave when I left the corporate world provided the foundation I needed to succeed in this business.

Al Hofacker and Jack Brauer: When no one had a clue who I was, you asked me to be one of *Deer & Deer Hunting's* first field editors in the early 80s. Thanks for giving me my first break in this business.

Al Brothers: Thanks for your QDM sales pitch in 1989. You truly are the father of QDM, and I count it an honor to call you a friend.

Pat Durkin: From your *Deer & Deer Hunting* editor's desk you let me write prolifically about QDM. Thanks for the many opportunities you gave me and for your friendship and encouragement.

Dan Schmidt: You're one of the most knowledgeable whitetail editors I've known. Our tenure with *Deer & Deer Hunting* has been a blessing. Thank you for your editorial guidance, whitetail wisdom and friendship.

Brian Murphy: Thank you for your tireless

efforts as executive director of the Quality Deer Management Association. Your guidance and salesmanship have furthered the cause of QDM more than you know.

Paul Daniels: Thanks to one of my best friends in the world. You've always been willing to do anything I've asked. The part you've played in Steuben County's QDM movement has been great.

Terry Rice: Thanks for the part you've played in our QDM program. Your help in managing our doe population has been special. But most of all, thanks for being a great friend.

Rob Roote: To a great neighbor, QDM advocate and leader of Steuben County's QDM movement. Your time and effort have been greatly appreciated.

Craig and Neil Dougherty: In many ways, we've learned QDM together. Our fireside chats and experiments with whitetail management have let us form a unique bond. It's been a great run.

Dr. Grant Woods and Dr. Mike Lormore: A special thanks to two of the brightest minds within the QDM movement. Your insight into the technical side of QDM has been incredible. It's great to have you as sounding boards and friends.

Bob and Alma Avery: Without your love and the opportunities you gave me to observe deer on your wilderness paradise, I might never have been able to learn what I have about white-tailed deer.

Ben Lingle: Thanks for giving me one of my first breaks in this business. Access to your estate gave me some incredible insights into the whitetail world.

Mike Biggs, Leonard Lee Rue III and Erwin Bauer: Collectively, you're the best whitetail photographers/writers in the world. Thanks for inspiring me and keeping my competitive fire lit. Most of all, thanks for being my friends.

George and Elizabeth Jambers: In many ways, your Texas ranch provided my first glimpse of QDM in action. You went out of your way to help this Yankee, and the love you showed me will never be forgotten.

Hefner Appling Sr.: Thanks for giving me a glimpse of QDM — Texas style. It was a real eye opener.

I offer a special thank you to Jennifer Pillath, my editor on this book. Your energy, keen mind and artistic skills will forever be appreciated. It was great working with you.

Tom Morgan and Dave Griffith: Thanks for sharing your whitetail insights. You are two of the best whitetail breeders in the business.

Jim, Charlie, Jack, Aaron, Paul, Whitey, Spook, Carla and Buttercup: Without you, I wouldn't have learned what I know about whitetails. Collectively you have taught me more than all the wildlife biologists or scientific journals combined. Thanks for giving me a window to the whitetail's hidden world.

Last, but most importantly, I want to thank Jesus Christ for the gift of life and the career field He has placed me in. He's given me the greatest job on earth and without His guidance and direction, this book wouldn't have been possible.

About the Author

Charles Alsheimer is an outdoor writer, lecturer, whitetail consultant and award-winning nature photographer from Bath, N.Y. Alsheimer was born and raised on a farm and has devoted his life to photographing, writing and lecturing about the wonders of God's creation. Alsheimer specializes in white-tailed deer.

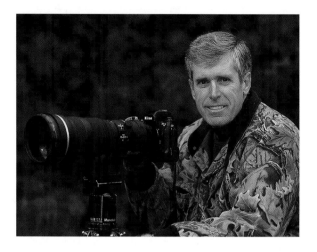

He is the northern field editor for *Deer & Deer Hunting* magazine and a contributing editor for *Whitetail News*. In the past 20 years, Alsheimer's work has taken him across North America. His photos have won many state and national contests, and his articles and photographs have appeared in nearly every major outdoor publication, including *Outdoor Life*, *Field & Stream*, *Sports Afield*, Harris Publications and *Deer & Deer Hunting*. In addition, he has written three popular books on the whitetail and co-authored a fourth. Alsheimer also owns and operates a white-tailed deer research facility and provides consulting services to various segments of the whitetail industry.

In a national poll conducted in January 2000 by *Deer & Deer Hunting*, Alsheimer was honored as one of deer hunting's top five inspirational leaders of the past century. The ballot included nearly 60 scientists, manufacturers, politicians, celebrities, communicators and hunters whose names are intertwined with deer hunting. Each had in some way increased America's understanding of the white-tailed deer, whether through the invention of camouflage patterns, the establishment of national forests or the writing of internationally known books. Alsheimer ranked third behind Fred Bear and Aldo Leopold, and ahead of fourth place finisher, President Teddy Roosevelt. This honor illustrates the respect Alsheimer has among deer hunters.

Alsheimer is an active member of the Outdoor Writers Association of America, the New York State Outdoor Writers Association and the National Rifle Association. He has also served as a nature photography instructor for the National Wildlife Federation at its Blue Ridge, Maine, and Nova Scotia Summits.

Alsheimer lives with his wife and son on a farm in rural upstate New York.